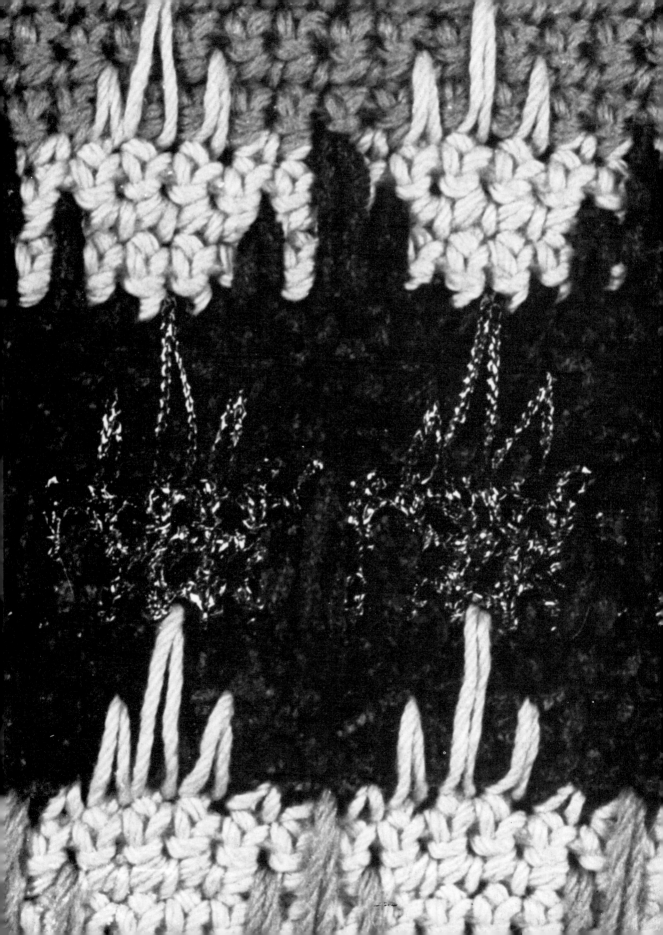

The Batsford Book of Crochet

The Batsford Book of
Crochet

Ann Stearns

B T BATSFORD LTD · LONDON

First published 1981
First published in paperback 1987
© Ann Stearns 1981

ISBN 0 7134 3313 2

Filmset in 10pt. Monophoto Apollo by
Servis Filmsetting Ltd, Manchester
Printed in Great Britain by
Anchor Brendon Ltd, Tiptree, Essex
for the publishers B T Batsford Ltd
4 Fitzhardinge Street London W1H 0AH

Contents

Frontispiece. Study for The Crochet Worker, Miss Mary Ann Purdon, *William Etty, 1849.*
City of York Art Gallery (G J Wolstenholme bequest)

Acknowledgment

My thanks are due to the following who have helped me with the making of many of the samples and projects in this book: Iris Campin; Molly Eagle; Dorothy Hall; Joan Morrow; Lesley Nash; Edith Radcliffe; Ivy Thompson; Jonathan Leach and Veronica Cox for allowing me to photograph their hand-spun yarns; Jean Mould for her fashion sketches in Chapter 18; Catherine Kay for her sketches in Chapter 19; Maxine Morrison and Lucy Stearns for modelling the outfits in the book and lastly my husband Bryan, who took all the photographs (except those with individual credits).

I would like to add my gratitude to the yarn manufacturers who supplied me with the yarns specially chosen for the projects: Patons and Baldwins Ltd; H G Twilley Ltd; The Coats Sewing Group; and Abel Morrall Limited for supplying the crochet hooks, Tunisian hooks and hairpin prongs.

My thanks also go to Thelma M Nye and Belinda Baker of Batsford for their help and encouragement.

I am grateful to the many Turkish friends who have so very willingly and patiently helped me with Chapter 19, Turkish Crochet, especially Nur Kaplan. My thanks are due to: Mügül Andrews and her mother, Nadide Uluant, Professor Kenan Özbel. I would like to thank Yildiz Arda from the Turco-British Association for introducing me to Nezihe Araz, who kindly showed me many articles of crochet from her personal collections.

The author and publishers would also like to thank the following for their permission to reproduce the illustrations used in this book: The City of York Art Gallery (GJ Wolstenhome bequest) (frontispiece); the Mary O'Donell Boutique (392); The National Museum of Ireland (393, 423); Patons and Baldwins Ltd (1); the Textile Institute, Manchester (4); the Trustees of the Rachel B Kay-Shuttleworth collections, Gawthorpe Hall (390, 391); the Victoria and Albert Museum (388, 394, 395, 397, 424); the Welch Collection, Ulster Museum (386); Whitworth Art Gallery, Manchester (387).

Introduction

Whilst the craft of crochet in its chain-stitch form has connections with the making of very early textiles and crochet as a fabric form became highly developed in Europe during the nineteenth century, interest in it lapsed to some extent until fairly recently. In recent years experimentation and the re-examination of old techniques have re-engendered an enthusiasm for crochet which has again become an extremely popular and widely practised craft.

The popularity of crochet undoubtedly stems from its wide range of application and achievement. At one level it is easily learned by children, who were taught it almost as a matter of course in the nineteenth century, whilst at the other end of the scale the skilled worker can produce most complicated and beautiful designs epitomized by the Irish crochet laces of the last century.

This book aims to provide the beginner with a sound basis by demonstrating the primary stitches and techniques which it is essential to master before more complicated and advanced work can be attempted. Step by step descriptions of stitches are both described and illustrated and the left-handed worker is catered for. Tunisian, filet and hairpin techniques are all covered.

It is, however, not the primary intention of this book to provide detailed patterns for the garments and accessories illustrated, as it is the author's belief and experience that most craftsmen, having learnt a technique, find it more rewarding to develop their own ideas and designs. Nevertheless, readers will find charted outlines which show how the garments illustrated were designed.

In order to encourage a broad appreciation of the craft, references are made to crochet from other countries. Whilst crochet techniques may vary only slightly from one country to another the essential difference in the work lies in the design and decoration. There is clear evidence in some work illustrated that ethnic motives and patterns were incorporated into crochet work as they were into other craft forms. Perhaps the best illustration of this is to be found in the fascinating work from Turkey, the Middle East and, particularly, Ireland.

Not only does crochet provide an absorbing craft in its own right but it presents a basis for experimentation and development at least equal to other craft forms.

A S
Horton-cum-Studley
1981

1   Crochet hook sizes July 1969 (comparison chart)

These hooks are shown in actual size with present as well as new international numbering. Throughout this book the new international hook size will be quoted. By permission of Patons and Baldwins Limited.

	New Range International	Present Range Steel	Present Range Disc (aluminium)
		8	
		7	
		$6\frac{1}{2}$	
	0.60 mm	6	
		$5\frac{1}{2}$	
	0.75 mm	5	
		$4\frac{1}{2}$	
	1.00 mm	4	
		$3\frac{1}{2}$	
	1.25 mm	3	
	1.50 mm	$2\frac{1}{2}$	
	1.75 mm	2	
		$1\frac{1}{2}$	
	2.00 mm	1	14
		1/0	13
	2.50 mm	2/0	12
	3.00 mm	3/0	11
			10
	3.50 mm		9
	4.00 mm		8
	4.50 mm		7
	5.00 mm		6
	5.50 mm		5
	6.00 mm		4
	7.00 mm		2

1 – Materials and equipment

Most crochet requires one piece of equipment – a crochet hook; one type of material – a continuous length of yarn, and very flexible fingers. All the materials used for crochet work are usually termed yarns. The yarn may be made from natural fibre – wool, cotton, linen or silk. Alternatively it may be made from man-made fibres or even a mixture of two or more different yarns. Crochet may be worked from any of the traditional yarns which are sold commercially, or indeed, from some more unexpected materials such as ribbon, tape, piping cord, rouleau strips, strips of cut fabric, string, wire, leather thonging and raffia. In fact any material which can be found in a long continuous length can be used for crochet work. It is fun to experiment with these more unusual yarns and see the results. The yarns sold commercially fall into two 'type' categories, irrespective of fibre content.

One type is the traditional, smooth yarn of one colour. The second type covers the fancy yarns, featuring colours and/or texture qualities. The smooth yarns are ideal for crochet as the textural qualities of the work are shown more clearly when using a plain smooth yarn. These yarns can be very fine, eg Coats No. 80 cotton mercer yarn, or at the other end of the scale, very thick, eg rug wool. The plying of yarns governs the thickness of the final yarn; one single ply can be used or several lengths twisted together. Again, the thickness of a single ply yarn can vary. However, different yarn manufacturers do not always produce the same thickness for the same plys. A 4-ply yarn made by one manufacturer may not be exactly the same as that made by another manufacturer.

The method in which the yarns are twisted together forming the various plys also affects the final yarn type, producing the fancy yarns. For example, different techniques in plying can produce slub yarns (yarns with thick lumps at various intervals), slub gimp yarns (as above but a wavy yarn), stripe yarns (yarns with elongated knops), knop yarns (yarns with prominent bunches of threads at various intervals), snarl yarns (yarns with twisted projections), loop yarns (yarns with wavy circular projections), gimp yarns (yarns with wavy projections on the surface), spiral yarns (yarns with an uneven twisted ply construction), bouclé yarns (yarns with irregular loops) and chenille yarns (tufted yarns).

Colour also plays an important factor when selecting yarns. Colour should always be related to the proposed situation and purpose of the article to be made. If you are making a garment for yourself, select a colour to emphasize your own colouring, ie your eye or hair colour. If the article is to be for the house, again think of the surroundings and let your colour choice fit in with the background. If selecting a number of colours for an article, think carefully *before* you are faced with the marvellous ranges of colour in the shops. Try for different tones of one colour or harmonizing tones such as browns, beiges, oranges.

When selecting a commercial crochet pattern, the yarn will be clearly stated. The manufacturers of the yarn, the type and amount required, the number of colours to be used, will all be included in the pattern. Do follow these instructions as disappointing results will occur if an incorrect yarn type is used. Always use the stated yarn for a given commercial pattern; always buy enough yarn and always try the tension sample before starting the actual project (see Chapter 17, page 105). However, if working without a commercial pattern and making your own design, it is well worth buying the best quality yarns; crochet work is very long lasting and the time used in making the article is precious, so you really do need a good quality, long lasting yarn for your work. Also, good materials are much more pleasing to work with. The best yarns will usually stand up to careful washing or dry cleaning – so disappointments will be avoided. The label on the yarn wrapper always states the yarn content and the washing instructions, and these should be observed.

Crochet hooks come in various sizes from 0.6 mm to 12 mm. Since 1969 these hook sizes have been standardized and include the different types and sizes which used to be available and cause some confusion. Many people still have the old hooks with the old number system, and figure 1 will help to clarify the sizes required for up-to-date instructions.

In addition to a good variety of yarns and the full range of hook sizes, other useful pieces of equipment which will be needed from time to time include a tape measure, a firm ruler, safety pins, scissors for cutting paper and fabric, a calculator, a full range of pressing equipment and pressing cloths, sewing equipment and needles of various types. For some of the various types of crochet suggested in this book you will need an embroidery frame, Tunisian crochet hooks (ie the very long hooks) in sizes 10 mm to 2.5 mm and hair pin prongs in the range of widths 10 mm to 100 mm. Large wooden knitting needles or dowelling to be used for a gauge when making loops will also be referred to in this book. Useful equipment for experimental work and designing garments includes fashion magazines and books on fashion for inspiration, drawing and sketching materials, such as paper, pencils and coloured felt pens, graph paper and a full length mirror for testing and evaluating results. It is most important to hold a piece of crochet fabric or to fit the toile (calico pattern of garment to be made) in front of a full length mirror in order to see if it is really suitable for you.

The relationship between the yarn and hook size is

of the greatest importance and will be directly governed by the article to be worked. Whatever you are making, and whether you are working a commercial design or making up your own design, it cannot be stressed too firmly that you should always work a trial sample for reference. The problem in crochet always seems to be the tension, ie the closeness of the stitches. These trial pieces are required to test the tension. The tension can vary from person to person and sometimes from one piece of crochet to another by the same worker. The ideal should, of course, be a really firm and above all *consistent* tension. This will produce a fabric of good technical quality and will be long lasting. For garments especially, firm and even tension is of the utmost importance. If the tension is poor and irregular, the garment will lose its shape, it will stretch and distortion of the outline will result. An incorrect

hook size is often the cause of poor tension. The suggested hook size is given for most commercial patterns and you should begin by using this stated size with the recommended yarn type. Produce your ·trial piece and check your work for tension (see Chapter 17 page 105). When designing your own projects, trial samples are just as important and test pieces should be worked as before and fully labelled. The rows and stitches should be counted over a set measure and noted. These figures will be your guide when starting the pattern shapes for your project. No guide can be given here for the correct suggested tension, but try the chosen yarn type with different hooks which you find workable, and experience will help you achieve a firm close tension in most instances.

The various articles which can be made using

2   A selection of hand spun yarns which have been dyed with vegetable dyes. This gives an interesting and exciting dimension to the process of choosing yarns for crochet. Great variety in colour and texture can be achieved, and very subtle shading which it is not always possible to obtain with commercial yarns. In the space available in this book it is not possible to give details on spinning and dying yarns, but good

reference books on these subjects are given in the Bibliography (page 158).

3   An Ashford spinning wheel, which makes an ideal wheel for people learning to spin for the first time. These wheels are available in kit form at a very reasonable cost from The Handweavers Studio and Gallery Limited in London.

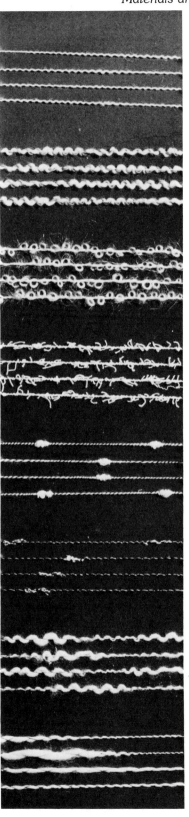

crochet include fashion garments and accessories, household articles, trimmings, cushions, floor coverings and wall hangings. Cords, fringes and tassels can also be worked in crochet. Three-dimensional work, sculptured articles, constructions and textured trimmings for embroidery as well as a base fabric for embroidery can all utilize crochet techniques. The scope is limitless, but it will be the choice of yarn which will make or mar the success of your project — always select your yarns thoughtfully and be thoroughly aware of its properties, especially if you are making a garment.

4 Fancy yarns. From the top: spiral, gimp, loop, snarl, knop, stripe, eccentric (slub gimp) and slub. From *Textile Terms and Definitions*, 7th edition, 1975, available from The Textile Institute, 10 Blackfriars Street, Manchester, M3 5DR. *By permission of the Textile Institute*.

5 A selection of treble stitch samples using: rayon tubular yarn, ribbon, chenille, Russian braid, string, raffia and plastic.

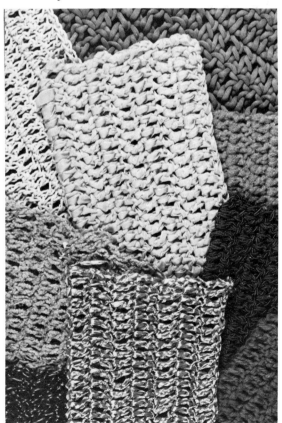

2 – Primary stitches and techniques

The primary stitches cover the chain, slip stitch, double crochet, half treble, treble, triple treble and quadruple treble stitches. At various stages I have included some of the difficulties I have encountered while teaching students to crochet. One of the biggest problems is the cry from left-handed people and I have, therefore, included photographs to help them in this chapter.

Crochet is usually a single yarn technique using one continuous thread like knitting, tatting and netting, in contrast to the multi-yarn techniques such as weaving, macramé and bobbin lace.

Before starting to crochet a fabric, a base foundation is usually required – this is known as the foundation chain.[1] The start of the foundation chain is a slip loop.

For all the explanatory instructions given in this chapter, I would suggest using a No. 5.00 ISR crochet hook and a double knitting yarn. Select a yarn with a smooth texture and a good twist – it can be difficult when learning the basic stitches to insert your hook cleanly through each stitch and avoid splitting the yarn. This will cause a poor fabric with weak spots.

Holding the yarn and the crochet hook

6   The right hand holding the hook. The barb is facing towards you and the second finger is controlling the hook along the back.

7   The left hand holding the yarn. The cut end of yarn should be towards you and the ball on the opposite side. Hold the yarn firmly between the thumb and first finger. Leave a space between the first and second fingers. Wrap the yarn around the fourth finger twice as shown. Keep the third and fourth

fingers close together as this will help you to control the flow of yarn from the ball. This is one method of holding the yarn – you may find alternative methods. However, whichever method you select, it is important to realize that it is the holding of the yarn supply from the ball of yarn which governs your working stitches, and ultimately your tension.

Making the slip loop

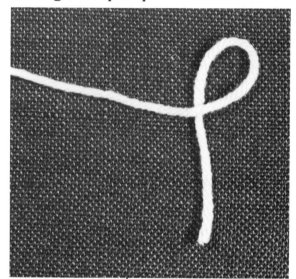

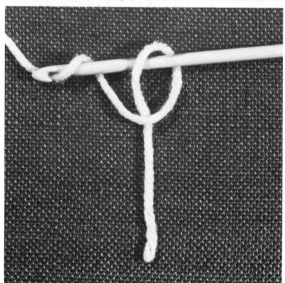

8 and 9   The start of the slip loop. Note that it is the yarn from the ball which is taken up to make the loop on the hook.

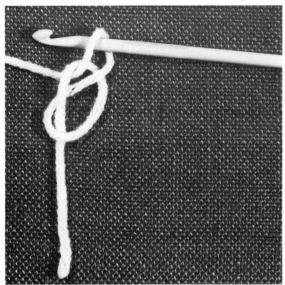

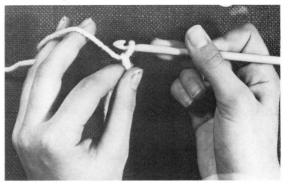

10 The slip loop is formed on the hook and when the yarn has been tightened on the hook you are ready to begin. This loop should not be pulled too tightly or you will have difficulty in working the following stitch.

Making a chain foundation

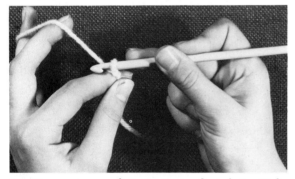

11 You are now ready to start your first chain stitch.

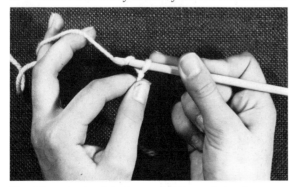

12 Place the hook in front of the yarn lying between the first and second fingers of the left hand, place the yarn over the hook and at the same time hold the yarn firmly below the hook with the left hand; this is referred to as yarn over hook (yoh).

13 Draw the yarn placed over the hook through the loop already on your hook. 1 chain stitch completed (1 ch).

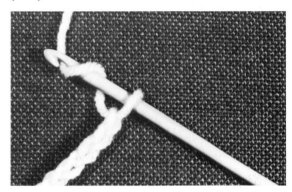

14 Continue repeating this technique for working a foundation chain.

15 It is important always to move the thumb and first finger of the left hand to a position immediately below the hook. By holding the yarn at this point, the worker can control the loop on the hook and this facilitates the working of the first chain stitches and all stitches following. It is most important that this motion should be mastered and a good technique achieved before learning the next techniques involved in crochet work.

Ending your work

When a length of chain is complete, or indeed any piece of crochet work, it is important to end your work by securing the last stitch very firmly. If the last stitch is left insecure, the work can be very easily and quickly pulled apart.

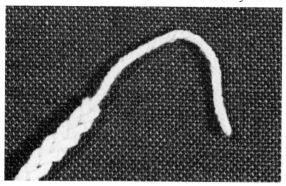

16   To end the last stitch, cut the yarn 25 cm beyond the hook – this gives enough spare yarn to thread into the work for neatening the finished yarn – and draw the cut end of yarn completely through the last loop on the hook. Pull yarn tightly to secure the last stitch. This method is always used to finish the work.

19   Right hand holding the yarn

(a)

(b)

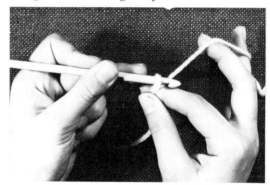

17
(a)   The working side or right side of a firm even chain length
(b)   A poor, uneven chain length
Chain stitch is a basic stitch and can be used as a main feature of a fabric, see the chain mesh, chain net and chain loops used for fabrics in the following chapters.

20   The position of the hands holding the hook and yarn with the slip loop on the hook

The left-handed worker
All instructions should be read transferring left for right, and right for left when referring to which hand is holding the hook and the yarn, except for the following six illustrations which are given exclusively for the left-handed person.

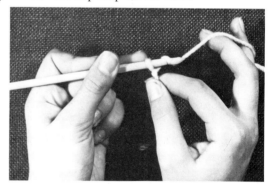

21   The first stitch – placing the yarn over the hook

18   Left hand holding the hook

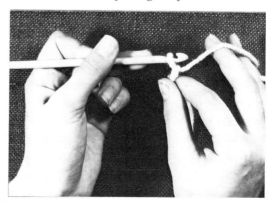

22   1 chain stitch completed

23   Working a chain length
Note the position of the right hand firmly under the working stitch.

Working onto your foundation chain

Crochet work can be, and usually is, worked to and fro like knitting – turning your work at the end of each row. Depending on the stitch pattern being used your work can have a right and wrong side or it can be completely reversible. Crochet can also be worked one way, which involves cutting the yarn at the end of each completed row; the work is not turned and the fabric will have a definite right and wrong side. The same effect is also achieved when working in circles – see Chapter 13.

When your foundation chain is the desired length, say 14 stitches, you are ready to learn the basic stitches. Usually these stitches are learnt in the order of their height, ie the depth of the completed stitch. However each stitch is a complete technique and you can start learning the stitches in a different order if you wish. The treble, double crochet or slip stitch can be learnt first. It is important to be able to work into your foundation chain with ease. Some people prefer to use a size larger hook for the foundation, and change to the required size hook for the following rows, for example, a size 5.50 ISR may be used for the chain foundation and a 5.00 ISR for the following work. Before working into your foundation chain decide which *hook insertion* method you prefer. Four variations are given, and a beginner would be well advised to try all four before selecting one method.

24   The hook is placed under the single top loop. *Note* the right side of the foundation chain faces you. This is a very popular method and easy to master.

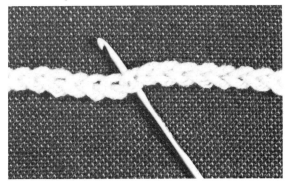

25   The hook is placed under the *2* top loops of the chain stitch. The right side of the foundation chain faces you. This method gives a very firm start to a piece of crochet fabric. It will be seen that the hook is really being placed under the *real* chain stitch which forms the basis of almost all the various crochet stitches.

26   The hook is placed under the single loop on the *reverse* side of the foundation. This again gives a firm start to a piece of work, but is more difficult to work.

27   The hook is placed under the *2* top loops on the right side of the chain foundation. This is not the same as figure 25. This is a very popular method chosen by many workers.

It must be stressed at this stage that when working into the foundation chain, care must be taken to avoid twisting the chain while working. If this happens an uneven and messy edge will result. The stitch count will be altered and this can cause difficulties if working to a special number of stitches. At all times, unless stated otherwise, you should always work into every chain stitch on a foundation.

Working the slip stitch (sl st)

At all times hold your work *immediately under* the stitch into which your hook is to be placed. This is most important and governs the control of the working of each stitch.

28   Insert the hook into the 2nd chain from the hook. *Note* the yarn forming the loop on the hook is not counted as a stitch. Count backwards from the hook (you will miss 1 chain stitch) and insert your hook into the next chain, ie the 2nd chain from the hook. Place the yarn over the hook noting the angle of the barb of the hook.

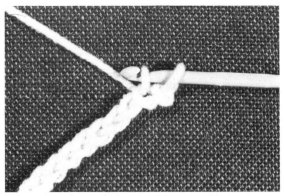

29   Turn the hook in order to pull the yarn through the foundation chain stitch.

30   Continue to pull the loop just made through the loop on the hook. 1 slip stitch has been completed.

31   Continue to work 1 slip stitch in each consecutive chain stitch. This example illustrates the hook placement being under the single top loop of each foundation chain as shown in figure 24.

The slip stitch is used for:
1   Making a fabric. See Chapter 5, and Chapter 19, Turkish Crochet. This is an unusual fabric – it is very close in texture and rather time consuming to work. However, various colours can be introduced which form most attractive patterns.
2   Probably the most usual purpose of the slip stitch is to move the working stitch along the fabric in order to achieve a shape, for example when constructing an armhole or neckline edge. By working along the fabric in slip stitch you avoid breaking the yarn and rejoining at the required position. The slip stitch is the only stitch suitable for this technique because it is the stitch with the least height.
3   Slip stitch is also used as a form of joining: either for crochet sections or motifs, or for completed sections of crochet fabrics.
4   Forming cords. Slip stitch worked along a foundation chain length forms an attractive and useful tying cord or belt.
5   Surface stitchery – see Chapter 12, page 81.
6   Surface stitching used as a neatening edging, as in the white Aran style sleeveless coat shown in colour plate 1 facing page 92.

Alternative method of working a foundation chain length – the double chain

Some people prefer to use the double chain as a method of working a foundation chain. This is a simple and easy technique to master. The foundation double chain also makes a useful cord.

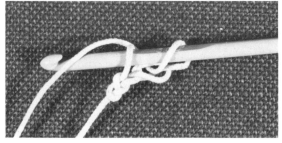

32   Work 2 chain. Insert hook under single top loop of the 2nd chain from the hook. Place yarn over hook.

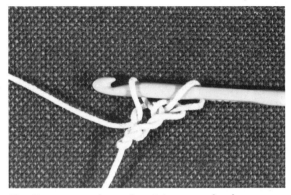

33 Draw yarn through – 2 loops on hook.

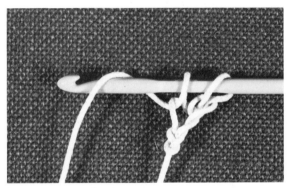

*34 Yarn over hook.

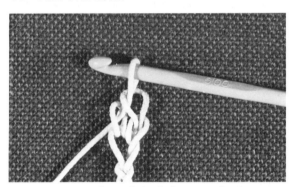

35 Draw yarn through both loops on hook.

36 Insert the hook under the single loop of the left-hand stitch just worked, place yarn over hook.

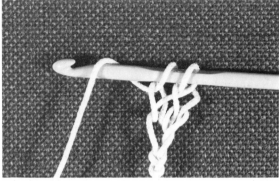

37 Draw through yarn – 2 loops on hook.*
Repeat instructions from * to * for required length.

38 Two foundations worked in double chain using different yarns.

The double crochet stitch (dc)
Work a foundation chain length, eg 15 stitches.

39 Insert hook into 3rd chain from hook – under both top loops.

40 Place yarn over hook.

41 Draw yarn through chain stitch – 2 loops on hook.

42 Place yarn over hook.

43 Draw yarn through both loops on hook. 1 double crochet stitch has been worked.
Continue to work 1 double crochet stitch into every consecutive chain stitch of the foundation.

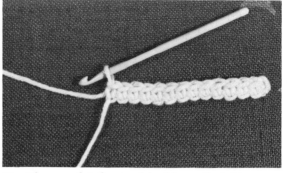

44 The completed row of double crochet. There are 14 stitches in total. The loop on the hook does not count as a stitch. It will be noted that although 15 chain stitches were worked for the foundation, 1 of these stitches forms the first double crochet stitch of the first row. It is important to remember this if working to a definite number of stitches.

Turn the work before starting the second row. It is advisable always to get into the habit of turning your work in the same way, that is, bring the right-hand side of your work towards you and place it on the left-hand side. This helps to give a good even edge to the fabric.

Row 2 45 Work 1 chain. This will form the first double crochet stitch of your second row. Work the next stitch into the 3rd stitch from the hook. The marker indicates the position for working this double crochet. Continue to work 1 double crochet stitch into every consecutive stitch of the previous row. The hook is placed under the 2 loops forming the 'chain' effect as noted in figure 25. This is the usual practice unless stated otherwise.

46 Second row of double crochet stitch complete. Remember to work 1 double crochet into the last stitch – this is the extra chain of the foundation row. Turn work.

47 Continue repeating the second row as shown in figures 45–46 until the required amount of fabric is complete. Six rows are shown in the illustration. When learning to crochet for the first time, it is advisable to count your stitches at the end of each row to ensure the number remains constant. The two main areas for mistakes are the first and last stitches worked. It is very easy to place the hook into the wrong position at the start of the row, and equally easy to miss the last stitch. These two problem areas should be thoroughly understood before proceeding onto more advanced stitches.

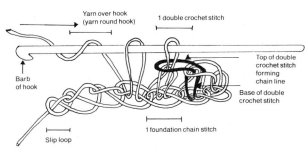

Hook placement as figure 27

48 Diagram to show the various parts and names of a foundation chain and the composition of the double crochet stitch. 7 chain stitches for the foundation chain length. 2 double crochet stitches have been worked, a 3rd started.

The half treble (htr)
Work a foundation chain length, eg 16 stitches.

49 Place yarn over hook.

50 Insert hook into 4th chain from hook – the marker indicates the position.

51 Place yarn over hook.

52 Draw yarn through the chain stitch – 3 loops on hook.

53 Place yarn over hook.

57 The last half treble stitch is worked into the 16th chain stitch of the foundation chain. Turn work and repeat the second row throughout. When learning this stitch for the first time, care should be taken to work the correct number of stitches for each row. A check count is recommended at the end of each row.

The treble stitch (tr)

Work a foundation chain length, eg 17 stitches.

54 Draw yarn through all 3 loops on hook. 1 half treble stitch has been completed.

58 Place yarn over hook and insert hook into the 5th chain from hook, yarn over hook and draw yarn through the chain stitch − 3 loops on hook.

55 Continue to work 1 half treble into every consecutive chain stitch of the foundation. The first row of half treble stitch is completed. There are 14 stitches in total. Again it should be noted that although 16 stitches formed the foundation chain, 2 of these stitches formed the first half treble stitch of your first row. 14 half treble stitches completed. Turn work.

59 Place yarn over hook.

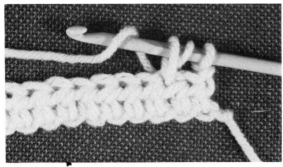

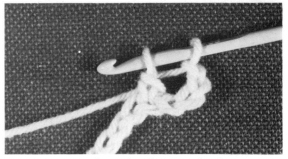

Row 2 56 Work 2 chain to count as first half treble stitch. Work 1 half treble stitch into the 4th stitch from hook. Work 1 half treble into each consecutive stitch of the previous row.

60 Draw yarn through 2 loops on hook.

61 Place yarn over hook.

62 Draw yarn through 2 loops on hook. 1 treble stitch has been worked. Continue to work 1 treble stitch into each consecutive chain stitch to end of foundation chain length.

63 14 treble stitches completed. Turn work.

Row 2 64 Work 3 chain to count as 1 treble. Place yarn over hook and insert hook into 5th stitch from hook as indicated by the marker.

65 Complete the treble stitch and work 1 treble into each consecutive stitch of the previous row.

66 The second row is complete – note the last treble is worked into the 17th chain stitch of the foundation chain. Turn work and repeat second row for required amount of fabric.

The double treble (dtr)

Work a foundation chain, eg 18 stitches.

67 Place yarn over hook *twice*. Insert hook into the 6th chain from hook.

68 Place yarn over hook and draw yarn through chain stitch, 4 loops on hook. Yarn over hook and draw through 2 loops. 3 loops left on hook.

69 Yarn over hook and draw through 2 loops on hook. 2 loops left on hook.

70 Yarn over hook and draw through 2 loops on hook. 1 double treble stitch has been completed. Work 1 double treble into each consecutive chain stitch.

71 14 double treble stitches completed. Turn work.

Row 2 **72** Work 4 chain to count as 1 double treble. Work 1 double treble into the 6th stitch from hook.
Work 1 double treble into each consecutive stitch of the previous row, ending with 1 double treble into the 18th chain of the foundation chain. Turn work.

Repeat the second row for required amount of fabric.

The triple treble (ttr)
Work a foundation chain, eg 19 stitches.

73 Place yarn over hook 3 times. Insert hook into the 7th chain from hook. Yarn over hook and draw yarn through chain stitch – 5 loops on hook. (Place yarn over hook and draw through 2 loops) 4 times. 1 triple treble has been completed. Work 1 triple treble into each chain stitch.

74 There will be 14 triple treble stitches. Turn work.

Row 2 **75** 5 chain to count as 1 triple treble. Work 1 triple treble into 7th stitch from hook. Work 1 triple treble into each stitch of the previous row ending with 1 triple treble in the 19th chain of the foundation

chain. Turn work. Repeat the second row for required amount of fabric.

The quadruple treble (quad tr)

Work a foundation chain, eg 20 stitches.

76 Place yarn over hook *4* times. Insert hook into the 8th chain from hook. Yarn over hook and draw yarn through chain stitch – 6 loops on hook. (Place yarn over hook and draw through 2 loops) 5 times. 1 quadruple treble has been completed.

77 Work 1 quadruple treble into each chain stitch – there should be 14 in total. Turn work.

Row 2 78 Work 6 chain to count as 1 quadruple treble. Work 1 quadruple treble into the 8th stitch from hook. Work 1 quadruple treble into each stitch of the previous row ending with 1 quadruple treble in the 20th chain of the foundation chain. Turn work. Repeat the second row for required amount of fabric. These stitch patterns form the basis of all crochet fabrics. They should be thoroughly mastered before progressing to more complicated work. Even longer stitches can be made, using the same methods and placing the yarn over the hook more and more times before taking the loops off in pairs.

It will be seen that all the basic crochet stitches, whether a chain, half treble or treble, etc are referred to as a *stitch*. This term covers any crochet stitch type which leaves a 2-loop chain effect along the fabric. The hook is then passed under these 2 loops unless stated otherwise. It will be seen that when working the stated pattern stitch after the *turning chain*, the hook is placed into the stitch with no turning chain above it. For clarity, when working in double crochet for example, this position is referred to as the 3rd stitch from the hook – the stitches in this example being 1 chain stitch, and 1 double crochet stitch. For the other stitches it will be seen that the number of stitches increases.

Table to show position for working the first pattern stitch

Double crochet	3rd stitch from hook
Half treble	4th stitch from hook
Treble	5th stitch from hook
Double treble	6th stitch from hook
Triple treble	7th stitch from hook
Quadruple treble	8th stitch from hook

These positions apply to the first row worked into a foundation chain, and all rows following.

At the end of each row, great care should be taken to place the last stitch of each row into the top chain of the turning chain. This is sometimes difficult to find and indeed it can be difficult to insert the hook. Missing this last stitch, and misplacing your hook after the turning chains at the start of the row are usually the causes of uneven edges, and loss or increase in the stitch count. When learning it is very advisable to count your stitches at the end of each row. Remember the turning chain(s) counts as one pattern stitch; the loop on your hook does not count.

Turning chains

Turning chains have been mentioned previously, but as they are so important special comment is required. While learning the basic techniques covered in this chapter, it will have been evident that when working crochet in the traditional manner, ie to and fro – turning your work for each new row so that you always work from right to left along your row – turning chains are required to start each new row. This serves to place the hook into the correct position above the last row worked. A turning chain consists of a number of chain stitches depending on the height of the stitch being used, ie 1 for double crochet, 2 for half treble. A table is given below.

Some people may find these stitches too long or too short, and you may need to alter the number depending on your tension and the type of work and yarn. These figures are given as a guide from which to start. Having worked the turning chain, it is important to be clear in your mind whether or not the turning chain is to count as a pattern stitch on the row – this is the usual procedure and governs the position for the next stitch.

Table to show the number of chain stitches forming the turning chains for basic crochet stitches

Double crochet	1
Half treble	2
Treble	3
Double treble	4
Triple treble	5
Quadruple treble	6

These figures also apply to the extra chains to be added to a foundation chain length in order to give a set number of stitches.

Two alternative foundations

At this stage you might like to try two different ways of starting your work. One gives a straight edge and the other method produces an attractive shell edge.

The straight edge method
Double treble chain foundation.

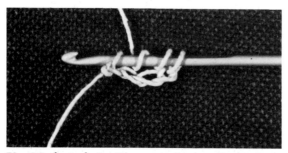

79 Work 4 chain. Yarn over hook twice as for a double treble. Insert hook into the 4th chain from hook.

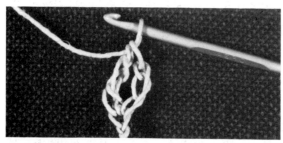

80 Complete double treble stitch.

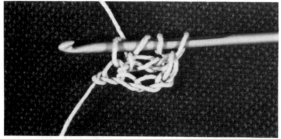

81 *Yarn over hook twice. Insert hook into the single loop at base of last double treble worked. Complete double treble in the usual manner.*
Repeat from * to *.

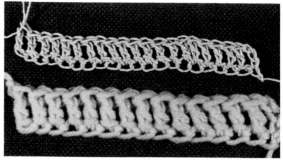

82 Two completed examples.
When the required length is made, turn work and continue working fabric placing hook into the top of each double treble stitch in the normal way.

Shell edge method

83 5 chain. 1 treble into the 5th chain from hook.

84 *3 chain.

85 1 treble into 4th stitch from hook.*
Repeat from * to * for required length.
Work the second row into the treble stitch, *not* the chain stitches, of this foundation.

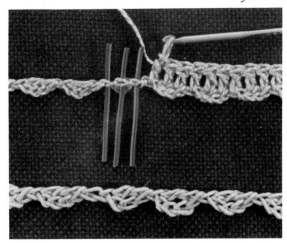

86 One completed shell edge foundation, and one showing treble stitches worked into the foundation. Three markers show where to insert hook. 3 trebles should be worked along each treble of the foundation. Insert hook under 2 loops each time.

Practising your stitches

Many variations of stitches can be achieved when these basics have been mastered. The main variations are made by:

   (a)   selection of hook size and yarn type
   (b)   method of hook placement
   (c)   number of times the yarn is placed round the hook
   (d)   the use of a gauge
   (e)   method of taking loops off hook
   (f)   the use of additional yarns and materials
   (g)   traditional (to and fro) or 'one way' crochet.

Some of these variations are shown in this chapter, and more appear in later chapters. Keep all your samples of stitch variations and patterns for future reference. Label each one saying what you did, the hook and yarn used. These samples will be very helpful when designing your own projects. In order to learn these variations it is as well to experiment at this stage. As a learning project, bags of any size make a good starting point. Cushions, scarves, stoles and shawls are also good practice. Patchwork squares and/or rectangles, being smaller pieces, may be your choice. All these articles can be made with straight edges and no increasing or decreasing is required. Also, the problems of correct tension (see page 105) are not so vital.

Figure 87 (a)–(n) shows some variations which were used for making small neck purses. These designs were worked over 20 stitches using Twilleys *Stalite* yarn and a No. 2.50 ISR crochet hook. Two pieces are required for each bag. Cords and tassels are added after the sides are sewn together.

All examples, except those marked † are worked in the traditional way, ie to and fro. Those marked † are 'one way' crochet – work two pieces of fabric breaking yarn at the end of each row, and not turning your work. A better technique would be to work over

40 stitches, in continuous rounds. This gives the same effect as the one way technique. Remember to work 1 slip stitch at the end of each round to join the last stitch to the first stitch of the round. Work the required amount of turning chains before starting the following round. There are more details about working in continuous rounds in Chapter 13, page 84.

87(a)   Basic double crochet stitch

(b)   Double crochet stitch †

(c)   Basic half treble stitch

(d)   Half treble stitch †

(e)   Half treble stitch. † Reverse side

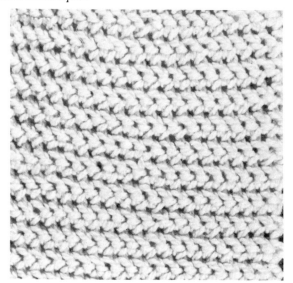

(f)   Knotted stitch †

Work into the foundation chain: yarn over hook, insert hook into 3rd stitch from hook, yarn over hook and draw through yarn and draw through 1 loop on hook. Yarn over hook and draw through both loops on hook. *Yarn over hook and insert hook into next stitch, yarn over hook and draw through yarn and through one loop on hook. Yarn over hook and draw through both loops on hook* Repeat from * to * to end of row. This row is repeated throughout.

(g)   Crossed double crochet stitch.

Into the foundation chain (uneven number) work:
Row 1   1 double crochet into 4th stitch from hook. 1 double crochet into chain stitch *before* last double crochet, so crossing hook in front of double crochet just worked. *Miss 1 stitch, 1 double crochet into next stitch. 1 double crochet into stitch missed*. Repeat from * to * to end of row. 1 double crochet into last stitch. Turn work.

Row 2 1 chain to count as 1 double crochet. 1 double crochet into 4th stitch from hook. 1 double crochet into stitch *before* last double crochet. *Miss 1 stitch, 1 double crochet into next stitch. 1 double crochet into stitch missed.* Repeat from * to * to end of row. 1 double crochet into turning chain at end of row. Turn work. Repeat row 2 throughout.

(h)   Counterpane stitch. Same as (f) but the work is turned, ie worked to and fro.

(i)   Slip stitch. † *Note* The hook is placed into the *single* back loop for each stitch worked.

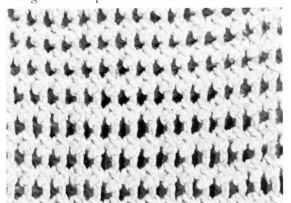

(j)   Double crochet variation †
Into a foundation chain work:

Insert hook into 3rd stitch from hook. Yarn over hook and draw through yarn. Insert hook into next stitch, yarn over hook and draw through yarn. Yarn over hook and draw through all 3 loops on hook. *Insert hook into same stitch as last hook insertion, yarn over hook and draw through yarn. Insert hook into next stitch, yarn over hook and draw through yarn, yarn over hook and draw through all three loops on hook*. Repeat from * to * to end of row. Repeat this row working 1 chain at start of round.

(k)   Double crochet variation. † *Note* The hook is placed under the single top back loop for each stitch worked.

(l)   Double crochet variation. † Sometimes known as Russian crossed stitch. The hook is placed *between* the 2 vertical loops on the right of the space for the usual position for the hook insertion.

Connected trebles (88–91)
Work a foundation chain.

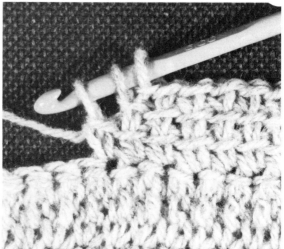

(m)   Connected trebles. † See figures 88–91. 3 chains should be worked at the start of each round.

(n)   Basic double crochet. Two yarn colours produce this design. Two rows are worked in each colour. All stitches marked † will have a right and wrong side to the fabric. This is an important feature when designing garments.

Insert hook into 2nd chain from hook, yarn over hook and draw through yarn, insert hook into next chain, yarn over hook and draw through yarn, insert hook into next chain, yarn over hook and draw through yarn, (4 loops on hook) (yarn over hook and draw through 2 loops) 3 times. *Insert hook under 2nd horizontal loop down of previous stitch, yarn over hook and draw through yarn. Insert hook under 3rd horizontal loop down of same stitch, yarn over hook and draw through yarn. Insert hook into next stitch on foundation, yarn over hook and draw through yarn (4 loops on hook – figure 88) (yarn over hook and draw through 2 loops) 3 times.* Repeat from * to * to end of chain. Turn work.

Row 2   Work 3 chain. Insert hook into 2nd chain from hook, yarn over hook and draw through yarn, insert hook into next chain, yarn over hook and draw through yarn, miss one stitch, insert hook into next stitch, yarn over hook and draw through yarn. (yarn over hook and draw through 2 loops) 3 times. Repeat from * to * of first row, working into treble stitches of previous row. Turn work. Repeat row 2 throughout.

93   The first step in making the double crochet

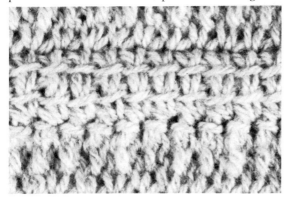

91   Two rows completed in connected trebles

Double crochet variation (92–94)

This is a mock ribbing. The double crochet stitch is worked in the usual manner inserting the hook under the single loop below the top of the double crochet worked on the previous row.

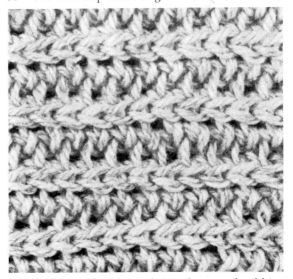

94   Sample of double crochet to form mock ribbing

Note   This technique is only successful for double crochet worked to and fro in the traditional manner.

92   The position for inserting the hook. A marker is shown in the correct position

Half treble variation (95–97)

This stitch is seen in the jumper illustrated in figure 108. This stitch is worked by placing yarn over hook, by taking the hook behind the yarn before inserting it into the next stitch; therefore the yarn is placed front over back and not back over front as in the normal manner.

95　The stitch: place yarn over hook as explained, insert the hook into the next stitch, yarn over hook and draw through yarn.

96　Yarn over hook and draw through all 3 loops on hook. Work 1 row in this stitch followed by 1 double crochet row.

97　A sample of half treble variation

Trebles in relief (98–99)

This stitch is seen in the jerkin illustrated in colour plate 2, between pages 92/3. The treble stitch is worked in the normal manner inserting the hook under the complete treble stitch of the previous row.

98 and 99　The working of the trebles for this pattern. A basic row of treble stitches is worked into the foundation chain before working this pattern.

Ridged double crochet (100–102)

The double crochet stitch is worked in the normal manner inserting the hook into the single back loop for every stitch.

100 and 101 The working of ridged double crochet. A basic row of double crochet stitches is worked into the foundation chain before working this pattern.

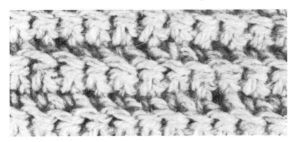

Cord stitch (103–105)

This stitch produces a very textured and knobbly fabric. The double crochet stitch is used throughout, but the work is *not* turned at the end of each row – nor is the yarn cut.

One row is worked in double crochet in the normal way, the next row is worked in double crochet, working from left to right.

103 and 104 The working of the cord stitch. On the return row in double crochet, the hook is inserted under the 2 loops between each pair of vertical loops of the double crochet of the previous row.

Increasing and decreasing

During the process of crochet, it will at some stage be necessary to shape your work by increasing the number of stitches worked in 1 row, or decreasing the number of stitches worked in 1 row. This is one of the basic techniques in crochet and should be understood before going on to more ambitious projects. Try each step before attempting a new technique. The cardigan illustrated in figure 209 features triangles made on the increasing technique. When shaping, there are two definite areas for increasing or decreasing: (a) on the edges or sides of the work; (b) in the main fabric of the work, ie in the process of working a row. Shaping on the edges can involve one or more stitches depending on the effect required.

Detailed explanations are given for working in double crochet and treble stitches, but the same process applies to all the other primary stitches.

Increasing in double crochet and treble – single stitches

Single stitches can be increased at any position in a row. However, when shaping on the sides of your work, it is better to work the shaping on the second or third stitches in, ie not on the very edge.

106 1 increased double crochet stitch. Simply work 2 stitches into 1 stitch of the previous row.

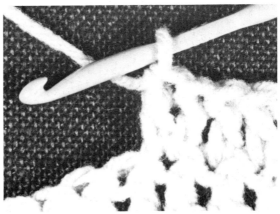

107 1 increased treble stitch. 2 stitches worked into 1 stitch of the previous row.

If more than 1 stitch increase is required, 2 stitches can be worked into 2 or more adjacent stitches.

To increase more than 1 stitch at the beginning of a row – double crochet

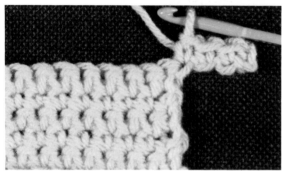

108 and 109   On the row where the increase is required, work the extra number of chain stitches required for the increase, plus the required number of turning chains to count as the first stitch, ie for a stitch increase of 4 stitches work 5 chain. Work 1 double crochet into 3rd chain from hook. Work along the added chain stitches and continue along row.

To increase more than 1 stitch at the end of a row – double crochet

110 and 111   There are several methods but the one illustrated proves the most straightforward. Use a

spare piece of matching yarn and join yarn onto the last stitch of the row where the increase is required. Work the required number of chain stitches for the increase and fasten off yarn. Continue along the row in the normal way, working over the extra chain stitches to give the increased shaping at the end of this row. A contrasting yarn is used for clarity.

To increase more than 1 stitch at the beginning of a row – treble stitch

112 and 113   On the row where the increase is required, work the extra number of chain stitches required for the increase, plus the required number of turning chains to count as the first stitch, ie for a stitch increase of 4 stitches work 7 chain. Work 1 treble into the 5th chain from hook. Work along the added chain stitches and continue along row.

To increase more than 1 stitch at the end of a row – treble stitch

114

114 and 115   An increase of 4 stitches in treble stitch. Use the same method as for double crochet.

Decreasing in double crochet and treble – single stitches

116 and 117   Avoid decreasing on the first and last stitches on the edges of your work. As with increasing it is best to work the shaping on the 2nd or 3rd stitches in from the edge, both at the beginning or the end of the row.

To decrease single stitches in double crochet, simply work 1 stitch over 2 stitches of the previous row, ie (insert hook into next stitch, yarn over hook and draw through yarn) twice, yarn over hook and draw through all 3 loops on hook.

118   Sometimes 1 stitch can be missed on the pre-

vious row to give a 1 stitch decrease. This is a quick and simple way, but can only be used on very closely worked crochet. A small hole is sometimes noticeable.

To decrease more than 1 stitch at the beginning of a row – double crochet

Slip stitch over the required number of stitches to be decreased. Work the required number of turning chains to count as the first double crochet stitch and continue along the row. For double crochet 1 chain forms the turning chain. The following double crochet is worked into the 3rd stitch from hook.

To decrease more than 1 stitch at the end of a row – double crochet

Mark the position where the decrease is to start at the end of the row and work to this point. Turn work and continue in pattern working the turning chain before working the next double crochet into the 3rd stitch from hook.

Decreasing in treble stitch

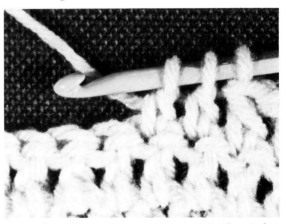

119   This follows the same process. Single stitches are decreased by working 1 stitch over 2 stitches of the previous row, ie (yarn over hook and insert hook into next stitch, yarn over hook and draw through yarn, yarn over hook and draw through 2 loops) twice.

120   Yarn over hook and draw through all 3 loops.

121 2 stitches can be decreased in treble by working 2 single decreased stitches over 4 adjacent stitches.

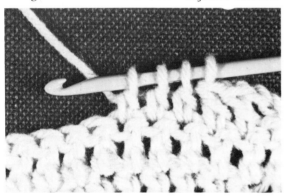

122 Alternatively, work 1 treble over 3 stitches.

123 Place yarn over hook and draw through all loops on hook.

To decrease more than 1 stitch at the beginning of the row – treble

Slip stitch over the required number of stitches to be decreased. Work the turning chains, ie 3 for treble, to count as the first treble stitch. Work 1 treble stitch into the 5th stitch from hook. Continue along row.

To decrease more than 1 stitch at the end of the row – treble

Mark the position where the decrease is to start at the end of the row and work to this point. Turn work and continue in pattern working 3 chains for turning chain, before working the next treble into the 5th stitch from hook.

Symbols and abbreviations

Symbols used in crochet

Chain (ch)	
Slip stitch (sl st)	
Double crochet (dc)	
Half treble (htr)	
Treble (tr)	
Double treble (dtr)	
Triple treble (ttr)	
Quadruple treble (quad tr)	
Groups	
Clusters	
Puffs and bobbles (ie several stitches worked into one stitch and held together with one stitch)	
Picot	
Crochet starts at this position	

American equivalents

UK	American
Chain	Chain
Double crochet	Single crochet
Half treble	Half double crochet
Treble	Double crochet
Double treble	Treble
Triple treble	Double treble
Quadruple treble	Triple treble

If you work your own designs I'm sure you will develop some of your own shorthand symbols – but do make a key or you may forget!

List of some standard abbreviations used in crochet plus American counterparts

The number of times the yarn is placed over the hook for each stitch type is shown in brackets

English terms	Abbreviated terms	American terms
approximately	approx	
beginning	beg	
chain(s)	ch(s)	chain(s)
centimetre(s)	cm	
decrease	dec	
double crochet	dc	single crochet
double treble (2)	dtr	treble
half treble (1)	htr	half double crochet
increase	inc	
quadruple treble (4)	quad tr	triple treble
quintuple treble (5)	quin tr	quadruple treble
repeat	rep	
right side of fabric (work)	RS	
slip stitch	ss or sl st	
space(s)	sp(s)	
stitch(es)	st(s)	
together	tog	
treble (1)	tr	double crochet
triple treble (3)	tr tr	double treble
wrong side of fabric (work)	WS	
yarn over hook	yoh	
also referred to as: yarn round hook yarn over		

3 – Advanced stitches

Experimenting with basic techniques to achieve different patterns and effects can produce some exciting fabrics. When the primary and basic work has been covered, it is fun to try different techniques and materials. Ideas are suggested in the following pages for you to work out and follow through, using some of the more unusual techniques. The samples can be worked in any yarn, but select a suitable hook size for the yarn chosen. Remember to label any completed samples for future reference.

Crochet patterns varying the number of times the yarn is placed over and taken off the hook

124   Make a chain length – multiple of 3 + 1.
Row 1   1 double crochet into 3rd chain from hook. 1 double crochet in each chain to end. Turn work.
Row 2   1 chain to count as 1 double crochet. 1 double crochet into 3rd stitch from hook. 1 double crochet into next stitch. *Yarn over hook, insert hook into next stitch, yarn over hook and draw through yarn, (yarn over hook, insert hook into same stitch, yarn over hook and draw through yarn) 3 times. Yarn over hook and draw through all 9 loops on hook. 1 chain. Miss 1 stitch. 1 double crochet into next stitch.* Repeat from * to *. Turn work. Repeat row 2 throughout.

Crochet patterns using alternative hook insertion positions

Surface crossed trebles

125 and 126   Crossed trebles are worked over and above 2 standard treble stitches. The crossed stitches can be placed in whatever design you choose.

To work a crossed treble stitch, work along your row until the position for the crossed stitch. Miss 1 stitch of the previous row. Work 1 treble into the next stitch. Work 1 treble into the stitch missed by placing your hook in front of the last stitch worked. The treble is worked directly *over* the vertical treble stitch and not into the top of the stitch (126).

Basket weave stitches

127–129   This is a variation of the last pattern. The basic stitch is treble, but the hook placement is *under* the complete vertical treble stitch of the previous row. It is first worked from the front, then from the back. Many designs can be worked using this technique. In the example shown a 4-stitch group has been used, ie 4 trebles worked from the front, 4 trebles worked from the back. Figure 128 shows trebles worked from the front and figure 129 trebles worked from the back.

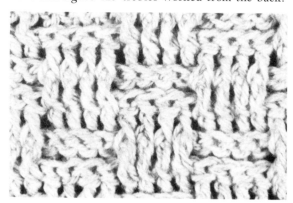

Crochet patterns worked by altering the stitch length

Three examples are given: (a) using a cut piece of card as a gauge; (b) using a large wooden knitting needle or piece of dowelling; (c) by extension.

(a) Fan stitch

130 and 131 Cut a piece of stiff card to be used as a gauge, eg 4 cm wide. Work along the row until the required position for the fan stitch. Place card along work with left hand and work a traditional treble stitch into the stitch of the previous row. The hook is placed in front of the gauge. 1 treble stitch can be worked or several – say 11 as in the example shown. It will be seen that this stitch is quite large and the fan shape opens out when the card is removed. Therefore several stitches can be missed on either side of the fan – in this example 5 stitches would be left unworked on either side. Many variations can be worked incorporating this fan stitch pattern. Figure 130 illustrates the use of this pattern using mohair yarn which is very suitable for shawls.

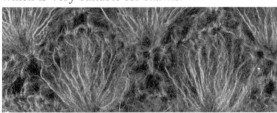

(b) Extended stitch crochet patterns using a large wooden knitting needle or other suitable gauge

132–134 Work the required amount of fabric in chosen crochet stitch before working the decorative row of extended stitches.

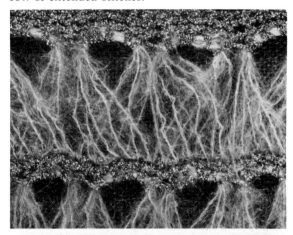

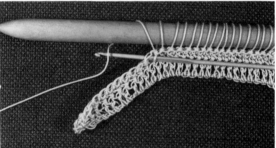

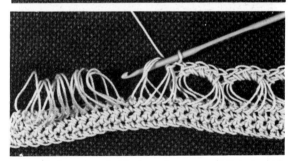

To work the extended loops, place gauge behind work and place yarn in front and over the top of the gauge to work a double crochet stitch along the row (133). Continue along row working in double crochet stitch over gauge. Remove gauge and turn work.

The second row of this pattern works over the loops made by the gauge. To start the row, either extend the loop on the hook to reach the top of the loops or work the appropriate number of chain stitches. This will depend on the size of the gauge. Work in double crochet inserting the hook in 2, 3, 4 or 5 loops together: 2 double crochet for 2 loops, 3 double crochet for 3 loops and so on (134). Figure 132 uses mohair yarn and Lurex glitter yarn with a 5 cm gauge working on the 5-loop grouping.

(c)   Solomon's knot stitch

135–138   This stitch forms an open lacey fabric. It may be worked solely for the fabric or may be worked between more solid areas of crochet stitches. To work a Solomon's knot stitch: extend the loop on hook to measure 2 cm.

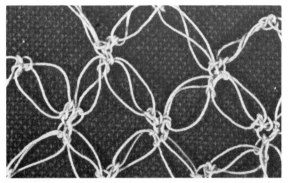

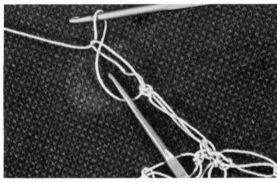

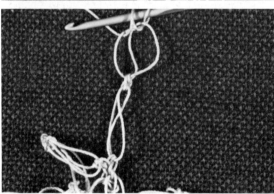

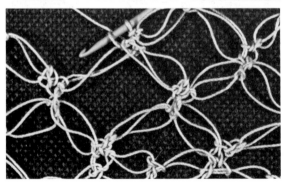

136   Insert hook into marked position.
137   Yarn over hook and draw through yarn (2 loops on hook), yarn over hook and draw through both loops on hook.
138   This stitch is often worked in pairs – the second Solomon's knot being joined between the 2 Solomon's knot stitches of the previous row. A double crochet stitch forms the join.

Crochet patterns combining different stitches

139   Trebles and chains
Make a chain length – multiple of 4 + 1.

Row 1   1 treble into 5th chain from hook. 1 chain. 2 treble into same chain stitch as last treble worked, *miss 3 chain, (2 treble, 1 chain, 2 treble) into next chain stitch.* Repeat from * to * to end of chain. Turn work.
Row 2   3 chain. *(2 treble, 1 chain, 2 treble) into next 1 chain space.*
Repeat from * to * to end of row. Turn work.
Repeat Row 2 throughout.

140   Treble groups and spaces
Make a chain length – multiple of 10 + 5.

Row 1   1 treble into 7th chain from hook. *1 chain, miss 1 chain, 1 treble in next chain.* Repeat from * to * to end. Turn work.
Row 2   3 chain. Miss 2 1-chain spaces. (ie 8 stitches). *9 trebles into next space. Miss 2 spaces. 1 treble into next treble. Miss 2 spaces.* Repeat from * to * until 3 spaces remain (ie 5 spaces left unworked because of the 2 spaces at the end of the repeat). 9 treble into next space. Miss 2 spaces. 1 treble in turning chain at end of row. Turn work.

Row 3 4 chain. 1 treble into 7th stitch from hook. *1 chain. Miss 1 stitch. 1 treble into next stitch.* Repeat from * to * to end of row. Turn work.

Rows 2 and 3 may be repeated throughout placing the groups of 9 trebles in vertical lines. Figure 140 shows the groups placed in line with the single treble stitch between the groups. Therefore, 4 rows would form this repeat pattern.

Crochet patterns combining different yarns

141 Twilley's *Capricorn* in grey. Twilley's *Lystwist* in gold. This fabric is featured in the two-piece suit illustrated in figure 367.

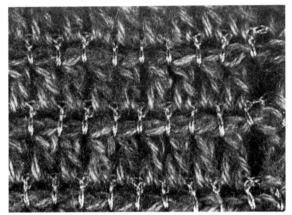

To work this fabric: work 1 row in trebles using a large hook size (7.00 ISR) and Twilley's *Capricorn*. Break off yarn and turn work.

Use a No. 3.00 ISR crochet hook and join in the *Lystwist* yarn between the first 2 trebles. Work 4 chain. *1 treble between the next 2 trebles, 1 chain.* Repeat from * to * to end of row. 1 treble in turning chain. Break off yarn and turn work.

Using the Capricorn yarn and a No. 7.00 ISR crochet hook, work in treble stitch, working each stitch into the chain stitch of the previous row.

Many variations can be based on this theme of mixing yarns, using the simple basic stitches.

Crochet patterns using the woven technique

To achieve a woven crochet fabric, a base material must first be made. To make a base fabric, select an appropriate yarn and hook for the type of fabric required, eg double knitting and a No. 5.00 ISR crochet hook. Make a chain length – multiple of 2 + 1.

Row 1 4 chain to count as 1 treble and one 1-chain space. 1 treble into 7th chain from hook. *1 chain, miss 1 chain, 1 treble into next chain.* Repeat from * to * to end of row. Turn work.

Row 2 4 chain to count as 1 treble and one 1-chain space. 1 treble into 7th stitch from hook. *1 chain, miss 1 stitch. 1 treble into next stitch.* Repeat from * to * to end of row. Last treble is worked into 3rd chain of turning chain. Turn work.

Repeat Row 2 for required amount of fabric.

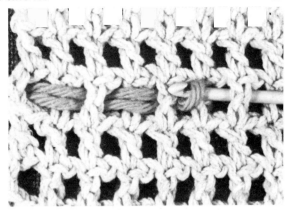

142 Contrasting yarns and/or ribbons are threaded through this base fabric foundation using a crochet hook. Place a hook over and under the vertical stitches and draw through yarns for horizontal weaving. The same process can be worked vertically. A Tunisian crochet hook is helpful for this process. Single or multiple groups of yarn can be used for the weaving process. Various permutations of over and under the vertical and horizontal lines can be worked using a variety of colours. The foundation base fabric can also be worked in stripes of different colours.

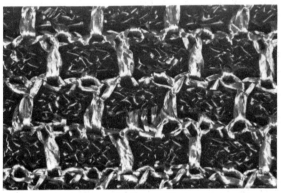

143 Base fabric worked in raffia. Horizontal weaving with a millinery braid.

144 Two colours form this sample: for the base fabric use each colour for alternate rows. The weaving is placed vertically – alternating colours again.

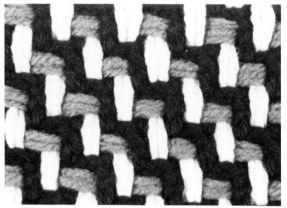

145   Three colours are used for this sample. The base fabric is worked in one colour. Vertical weaving in another colour, and horizontal weaving in the third colour.

146   A different base fabric is used for this sample. Double treble stitch forms the base. There are no chain stitch spaces. The weaving is worked horizontally using a petersham ribbon the same depth as the double treble stitch. The ribbon is placed over 3 stitches and under 3 stitches alternating the sequence for each new row.

Crochet patterns using two colours to give 'check' materials

147   Using colour A make a chain length – multiple of 6 + 1. Work 3 rows in double crochet placing hook

into the back single loop of each stitch of previous row (place first double crochet into the 3rd stitch from hook). The fabric is not turned and the yarn is cut and secured at the end of each row. The yarn is rejoined at the start of each new row working 1 chain stitch to count as 1 of the double crochet stitches.
Change to colour B. *Work 3 double crochet as before. Work 1 treble placing hook into the front loop of the next stitch in the third row below. Work 1 treble into the next 2 stitches in the same row below.* Repeat from * to * to end of row. Break off yarn and secure. Work 2 rows in double crochet working into the back single loop of each stitch of previous row.
Change to colour A. Repeat the last 3 rows to make the sample illustrated. Many interesting and attractive fabrics can be made using this technique. Experiment by changing the yarns, the colours, the number of rows worked between the row with the trebles, and the positioning of these trebles.

148   Colour A. Make a chain length – multiple of 2 + 4. Work 1 row in double treble stitch (place the first double treble into the 6th stitch from hook). Break off yarn, secure and turn work.
Colour B. Join to first stitch. 1 chain to count as 1 double crochet. Miss the chain stitch just made, 1 double crochet in each stitch to end of row. Break off yarn, secure and turn work.
Colour A. Join to first stitch. 3 chain. Insert hook under the double treble stitches of the second row below: Miss chain stitches at start of row, and *work 1 double treble under next double treble working from the front of the crochet. Work 1 double treble into next treble stitch working from the back of the crochet.* Repeat from * to * to end of row and the turning chain is left. Work 1 treble into the turning chain. Break off yarn, secure and turn work. Repeat the last 2 rows alternating the front and back working of the double crochet stitches.
This crochet pattern also looks very effective worked in one coloured yarn. This would eliminate the need to break off yarn at the end of each row.

Crochet patterns using different coloured yarns and inserting hook in rows below the usual top row to form zig zag designs

Further fabrics can be made by inserting the hook right through the fabric, from front to back and drawing the yarn through the crochet at different levels. The stitch used is double crochet – a firm close textured stitch is essential.

149 A fabric worked in double crochet, inserting the hook at 4 different levels: the hook is working the double crochet stitch into the top of the 4th row down.

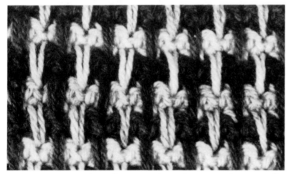

150 Four colours illustrated in this sample – working 2 double crochet rows in each colour. 1 double crochet stitch is placed into the 3rd row down on every alternate stitch.

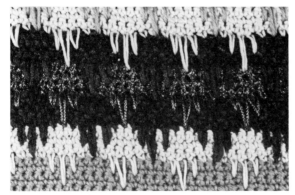

151 Four different yarn types and colours are used

in this sample – 4 double crochet rows in each yarn working 3 double crochet stitches into the top of the row, followed by 3 double crochet stitches worked into the 3rd, 4th and 3rd row down.

This technique is very versatile, and should lead to many individual patterns.

Crochet patterns using various colours to form chevron designs

Further variations are made to give a chevron effect by increasing and decreasing stitches in the same row. The same number of stitches are increased and decreased at set intervals so the stitch count remains constant. The fabric is usually formed by working in double crochet. Sometimes, other basic stitches are used. When working in double crochet, the hook is usually placed into the single back loop of the stitch of the previous row. This gives an added ridge to the chevron line.

The chevron line is formed by working a set number of stitches in double crochet, an increase of 2 stitches (ie work 3 double crochet into 1 stitch), followed by another set number of stitches in double crochet, and a decrease of 2 stitches (ie work 1 stitch over 3 stitches). On following rows the increased stitches are always worked over the increased stitches of the previous row, and the decreased stitches are worked over the decreased stitches. The number of single double crochet stitches worked between each increase and decrease can be the same, or the number can vary on the same row, but should be repeated exactly on following rows.

4 – Textured effects

Textured crochet stitches are used to produce loops, clusters, groups, pile fabrics, and crinkled surfaces. Several different techniques are explained; some of the methods give similar effects but you may find some techniques easier to follow than others. Sometimes, the choice of yarn or the article to be made will determine the method chosen.

Each textured stitch pattern explained can be made separately, in groups of rows or stitches, or as a complete fabric. Many of the textured effects are suitable for borders, such as hemlines, edgings for jackets and coats, cuffs and decorative panels combined with a plain smooth pattern stitch. For most of these textured fabrics, a plain and fairly smooth yarn type is best. All these textured fabrics have a right side and a wrong side – this is an important fact when making up a garment when you have a right-hand side and a left-hand side to make. The shaping must be placed on the appropriate edge. Because of the manner in which these stitches are made, a great deal of yarn is required and this adds to the weight of a garment. If the textured effect is to be placed, for example, on the front edge and hemline of a coat, it will be necessary to place a 'stay' thread along the line of the edging to prevent dropping and an uneven hemline. This is explained in detail in Chapter 17, Working methods.

Crochet textures made by placing extra long stitches next to very short stitches

152 This surface textured fabric is made up by working 4 quadruple trebles followed by 4 double crochet stitches. One row of double crochet is worked between the textured rows. The position of the quadruple trebles can be varied, as can the grouping of these extra long stitches.

153 This is a very long stitch which could be worked

in place of the quadruple treble. The yarn is placed 7 times over the hook before inserting the hook into the stitch of the previous row. This is followed by placing yarn over hook and drawing off 2 loops 8 times in the usual way.

154 An all over pile fabric worked in this technique, ie 1 stitch double crochet, 1 stitch formed by 7 overs as shown in figure 153. One complete double crochet row is worked between the pile stitch row.

155 and 156 Chain lengths are used to form this pile surface. The technique involves working 2 rows into 1 row – this gives a closer pile fabric than the previous example. Work several rows in a basic stitch before working the pile stitch row. The pile stitch row is worked: *7 chain, slip stitch into next stitch after the 7 chain stitches just worked – working into the *single back loop* of each stitch (155).* Repeat * to * to end of row. Turn work. On the return row work a normal row of double crochet placing the hook into the missed single back loop of the stitch when working the chain loop row. This technique can be worked as an all over fabric, or just for selected areas of a design.

Crochet textures formed by horizontal threads

These stitches are worked individually and may be worked in isolated areas to form a pattern on the crochet fabric, or in groups, or as a complete area.

157 Bullion stitch. This is rather a difficult stitch to work and requires practice. To work bullion stitch: place yarn over hook 8 times, insert hook into next stitch, yarn over hook and draw yarn through and through *all loops* on hook. The loops should lie firm and even, forming a smooth roll. Bullion stitches may be worked in adjacent stitches, or they may be separated by a chain stitch and missing one stitch on the previous row before working the next bullion stitch.

158–161 Block stitch. At the start of a row work 3 chain to place the hook at the correct height for this stitch. The block stitch may be worked at this position, or several treble stitches may be worked before the textured stitch.

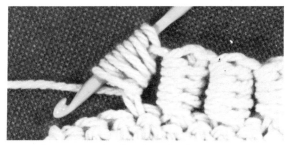

158 *(Yarn over hook, place hook in front of chain length, yarn over hook and draw the yarn up in front of chain length, yarn over hook from behind chain length) 4 times.

159 Insert hook into next stitch of previous row, yarn over hook and draw through yarn and through *all loops on hook.*
Note Keep this stitch quite loose on the hook in order to allow the loop of yarn on the hook to extend to the stitch length and reach to the top of the row.

160 Insert hook into next stitch, yarn over hook and draw through yarn.

161 Work 2 chain, yarn over hook and draw through both loops on hook.*
Repeat from * to * for block stitch.

It should be noted that if the block stitch is being worked after a series of treble stitches, the yarn is placed around the treble stitch previous to the block stitch, as there will be no chain length at this position.

Crochet textures formed by groups of vertical threads

Four different techniques are described – each one can be used as an isolated stitch, or in groups to form a stitch pattern, or for complete areas.

162–165 A tatted picot. This stitch requires practice, and should be placed between one or several stitches worked in double crochet.

162 Place yarn over hook as shown in the diagram 166, 8 times.

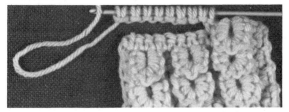

163 Loop yarn over hook (note the extended yarn on the left).

164 Draw through all loops on hook. The loops should be evenly spaced on the yarn.

165 Work 1 chain stitch. Miss 2 stitches of previous row, work 1 double crochet in next stitch. At least 1 row of double crochet should be worked before working another row with the tatted picots. There is, of course, a right and wrong side to the crochet fabric.

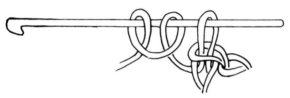

166 Diagram to show the method of placing the yarn on hook for making the tatted picot

167 Popcorn stitch. This textured stitch is formed by working a group of trebles, double trebles or deeper stitches into *1* stitch of the previous row. Popcorn stitch is worked singly or in groups. This stitch should be worked with stitches of the same height, ie a popcorn stitch worked in treble stitches should be placed in a row worked in treble stitches. To work 1 popcorn stitch: work 6 (can be more) trebles into 1 stitch of previous row. Remove hook and place into the 6th stitch back from working stitch. Place working stitch on hook and draw through work – thus closing the group of trebles together. On the return

row, which could be single treble stitches, care should be taken to work into all stitches forming the popcorn stitch in order to keep the stitch count constant. There is a definite right and wrong side to this crochet fabric.

168 Cluster or bobble stitch. This is formed by working several stitches into *1* stitch of the previous row, but the last loop of each stitch is retained on the hook forming a tighter grouping of stitches than the last example. This stitch can be worked singly or grouped, a row of plain double crochet usually separates a textured row, and therefore there is a definite right and wrong side to the crochet fabric. To work this cluster stitch: (Yarn over hook and insert hook into next stitch, yarn over hook and draw through yarn. Yarn over hook and draw through 2 loops), repeat 5 more times working into the same stitch position. Place yarn over hook and draw through *all* loops on hook. Work 1 chain stitch and miss 1 stitch of the previous row before working another cluster stitch.

169 Pine stitch. This is yet another type of clustered stitch. This textured stitch can be worked on every row – not alternate rows as the previous stitch patterns; it therefore has the advantage of appearing the same on both sides of the crochet fabric. A treble stitch is usually worked between the pine stitch. To work pine stitch: (place yarn over hook, insert hook into next stitch, yarn over hook and draw through yarn extending the loop of yarn to the treble stitch height). Repeat 6 times working into the *same* stitch position. Yarn over hook and draw through all loops on hook. 1 chain, miss 1 stitch before working another pine stitch. When working several consecutive rows, the pine stitch can be worked into the chain stitch of the previous row. It is best to work 1 or more trebles at the start and end of a row using this stitch.

Crochet textures forming looped pile fabrics using one yarn

A looped pile texture can be worked by using a rule or similar gauge consisting of a piece of firm card cut to the required fringe depth. There are two main techniques: (a) using the base yarn to form the loops, (b) using a second yarn to form the loops. Both techniques can be used to produce a single row of loops or may be placed repeatedly to give an all-over pile texture.

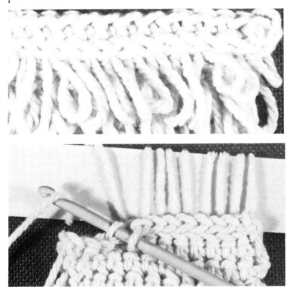

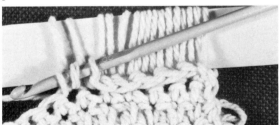

170 and 171 A very firm looped pile which tends to lie downwards. Because of the technique used, the loops do not pull out of shape as easily as some other types of 'piled' work. The base fabric is double crochet.

To work the loops: cut a gauge in firm card, 3–5 cm wide depending on the width of loop required. Place gauge along the row on the back of crochet – this will be the right side of your fabric. *Place yarn over top of gauge, insert hook into next stitch (placing hook into back single loop), yarn over hook (171) and draw through yarn and through loop on hook, ie 1 slip stitch.* Repeat from * to * to end of row. Remove gauge, and turn work. On the return row, work in double crochet placing the hook into the back single loop of slip stitch, and through the loop missed on the previous row.

172 A looped pile fabric which forms either a single loop or double loop. The base fabric is double crochet. To work the loops: place gauge along the row on the back of the crochet – this will be the right side of your fabric. *Place yarn over gauge, front over the top to the back, insert hook into next stitch, yarn over hook and draw through yarn. Yarn over hook and draw

through 1 loop on hook. Place yarn over gauge, insert hook into the same stitch, yarn over hook and draw through yarn (3 loops on hook). Yarn over hook and draw through all loops on hook.* Repeat from * to * to end of row. Remove gauge, turn work and work 1 double crochet row before repeating the loop row. If a single loop is required, omit the second yarn placement over gauge before completing the stitch.

Crochet textures forming looped pile fabrics using two or more yarns

Two yarns are required for these textures, one for the base fabric and one for the loops. By using this technique, different coloured yarns can be used to form the loops. Also the loops may be cut to give a cut pile texture. Several thicknesses of one coloured yarn or several different colours can form the loops.

173–175 A cut pile fabric. Rug wool is used for the sample to give a very firm pile, with a chunky yarn for the base fabric.

Work in double crochet stitch throughout. To work the pile: cut rug wool into lengths 7–9 cm long. With wrong side of the crochet fabric facing towards you, place three lengths of rug wool with the middle of each length against the last stitch worked. Insert hook into next stitch, yarn over hook and draw through yarn

Wrap the two strands of rug wool over the gauge, front over back, and work 1 double crochet stitch into the next stitch. At the same time place hook on right-hand side of rug wool from gauge as you work each double crochet stitch (177). A row of double crochet is usually worked between each pile row. This is an easy and quick stitch to work and is most effective if contrasting colours are used. The loops may be cut, but an iron-on non-woven interfacing should be ironed onto the wrong side of the crochet to prevent the pile coming out.

Twist the cut yarn as shown (175) – yarn over hook and draw through both loops on hook (ie complete the double crochet stitch). Place all cut ends of rug wool towards the right side of the fabric before working the next pile stitch.

176–177 Two yarns are required for this looped pile fabric – two strands of rug wool for the pile and a chunky yarn for the base. A gauge of the required loop depth (3–5 cm) is placed along the row, with the wrong side of the crochet fabric towards you while working.

5 – Cords, braids, edgings and fringes

Decorative cords, edgings, trimmings and fringes all form part of crochet technique. When designing your own articles it will sometimes be necessary to make additional trimmings as part of the design.

Crochet cords

Cords are suitable for ties, draw strings, belts and strings for bags. Some cords can be used as a decorative braiding, sewn onto the style line of a design in order to highlight the shape. The type of cord made will ultimately depend on the type of yarn used for the technique. Whenever decorative trimmings are used, it is imperative that they form an integral part of the finished design – the trimming should never appear to be 'put on'.

178 and 179   A firm cord which may be used as a trimming braid or to form a fabric – see Chapter 6.

To work the cord: Work 2 chain. 1 double crochet into 2nd chain from hook. Turn work. 1 double crochet in 2nd stitch from hook (this is quite difficult to find!). Turn work. *1 double crochet in 2 loops on left of work Turn work.* Repeat from * to * for required length. Practice is required to achieve an even cord. Points to watch are:
(a) Always turn work right to left.
(b) Keep the stitches fairly loose.
(c) Never split the yarn.
180   An even round cord using a *lucet* or *chain fork*.

This tool is similar in shape to a lyre, measuring approximately 9 cm from top to bottom. Older models vary in size. Sometimes old lucets can be purchased, or a copy of an old example made in plywood like the one shown in the illustration. There is a hole at the base of the prongs through which the cord is held as it is made. Alternatively, two crochet hooks can be used,

placed back to back with the barbs facing outwards. An old wooden cotton reel with two tacks placed opposite each other on either side of the centre hole make yet another substitute for a lucet. To make the cord: make a slip loop using the yarn towards the cut end, and place loop on left-hand prong. The cut end of the yarn is placed through the hole from back to front. The base of the slip loop should lie in the centre of the lucet. Hold the lucet in the left hand. Place yarn in front of right-hand prong and behind it. At the same time turn lucet so that the yarn is placed over the slip loop which is now on the right-hand side. Using a small size crochet hook, lift the slip loop over the yarn above it. Pull yarn tightly through the hole to tighten the loop below the prong. *Place yarn behind left-hand prong, turn lucet right to left so that yarn is placed above loop on right-hand prong (180). Lift loop on prong over yarn above it. Tighten stitches by pulling cord through hole, so that the cord is firm and lies in centre of lucet.* Repeat from * to * for required length of cord. This cord needs practice.

This cord may also be worked *without* rotating the lucet. Place yarn round prongs from front to back on each side – so making a figure of eight movement. Lift the stitch on the prong over yarn above for each yarn placement. This crossing over of yarn in the centre of the cord makes a very firm cord. A third cord is illustrated in Chapter 11, figure 278 where it is used on a quilted bag. This is the traditional twisted cord. To make a twisted cord: take several lengths of yarn and twist very tightly in an anti-clockwise direction (ie a Z twist). Halve the cord, and the yarns will twist back on themselves in a clockwise direction (ie a S twist) – forming a firm round cord. The ends must be secured to prevent the twist undoing. As a guide, a 1-metre length of twisted yarn (ie length before twisting) will produce a final twisted cord of 36–40 cm depending on the yarn used and the tightness of the twisting. The yarns used for this cord may be different in weight and colour, any number of yarns being used for the initial twisting.

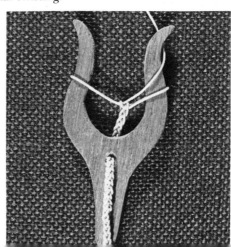

Small crochet edgings – some introducing picots

Edgings worked in crochet may be worked directly onto a crochet fabric, or they can be worked separately and sewn onto the fabric.

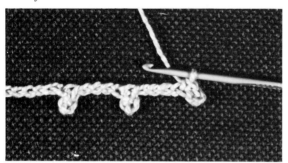

181   A simple narrow edging incorporating a picot. To work a picot: Work 4 chain followed by 1 double crochet stitch into the 4th chain from hook. Several chain stitches are worked between picots. Other basic crochet stitches may be worked in place of chain stitches to form an edging.

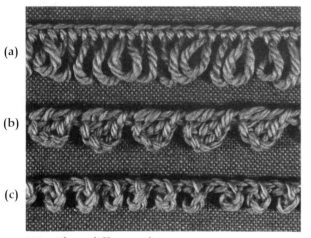

(a)

(b)

(c)

182   Three different edgings:
(a)   Looped edging. Work 2 chain. Extend loop on hook to required length (eg 3 cm). Remove hook. *Insert hook into 2nd stitch from extended loop, yarn over hook and draw through yarn. 2 chain, extend loop as before, remove hook.* Repeat * to *. *Note* The stitch just below the extended loop should be pulled tightly to secure the loop. Extended loops may be placed onto a gauge to form loops of an even length. Remove gauge when covered with loops.
(b)   Scalloped edging. *5 chain. 1 treble into 4th chain from hook. 1 treble in next chain.* Repeat from * to * for required length.
(c)   Twisted picots. 7 chain. *Insert hook into 5th chain from hook, work 7 chain.* Repeat * to * for required length. *Note* As the hook is placed back into the 5th chain, allow the picot to turn in an anti-clockwise circle. Place yarn over hook and draw the yarn through the chain stitch and through the loop on your hook, thus working 1 of the 7 chain stitches.

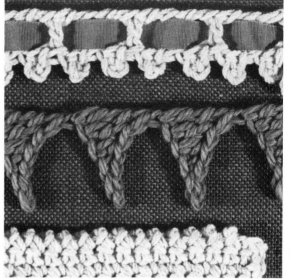

183   Three different edgings:
(a)   3 chain, 1 picot worked in the same way as shown in figure 181. Miss the picot and 2 chain stitches, work 1 quadruple treble into the next chain stitch. (ie the first chain stitch worked). *1 picot. 1 quadruple treble into the second twist of the last quadruple treble worked.* Repeat from * to * for required length. The quadruple treble forms both the sewing on edge and the vertical bar. Petersham ribbon can be threaded through the vertical bars for added effect.
(b)   Pointed edging. *Work 6 chain, 1 slip stitch in 2nd chain stitch from hook, 1 double crochet in next stitch, 1 half treble in next stitch, 1 treble in next stitch, 1 double treble in next stitch.* Repeat from * to * for required length. Try varying the stitch depth, ie work 8 chain and work correspondingly deeper stitches as you progress along the chain length.
(c)   Corded edging, also referred to as shrimp stitch. This edging is worked directly onto an existing crochet fabric. The stitch is worked from *left to right* in double crochet stitch. Place hook in front of work and insert into next stitch, yarn over hook and draw through yarn taking hook in front of work and twisting in a clockwise direction. Yarn over hook and draw through both loops on hook. Refer to Chapter 2, figures 103 and 104.

Crochet braids

Braid is used in this book to refer to a length of crochet which can be applied onto an existing fabric to emphasize style lines and certain design features, such as pockets. The braid usually has two straight edges which are the same. Many braids can be used as belts and straps etc.

184   A braid featuring a crossed effect. Three rows form the pattern. Work 1 row in double crochet. The next row forms the crossed effect by working connected triple trebles. At the start of this row work 5 chain stitches in order to place the crochet hook at the required height. (The 5 chain stitches worked at the

start of this braid count as a triple treble stitch, and the next hook insertion should be placed into the 7th stitch from hook.) To work a connected crossed triple treble: yarn over hook 3 times. Insert hook into next stitch, yarn over hook and draw through yarn, (yarn over hook and draw through 2 loops) twice. Yarn over hook, miss 1 stitch, insert hook into next stitch, yarn over hook and draw through yarn (5 loops on hook). (Yarn over hook and draw through 2 loops) 4 times. 1 chain. 1 treble into centre of cross to complete the cross. Work 3rd row in double crochet. Petersham ribbon may be threaded through the open spaces – over and under the crosses.

185   Two braids are twisted together to form this sample. Similar yarns or different yarns may be used. To work one braid: work a chain length twice the required length of braid. Work 1 double crochet into 3rd chain from hook. *1 double crochet in next 2 stitches, 3 double crochet in next stitch, 1 double crochet in next 3 stitches, decrease 2 stitches over next 3 stitches.* Repeat from * to * to end of chain length. Make a second braid in the same way, and twist the two braids together as shown in the illustration. Different stitches can be used for the zigzag braid such as half trebles and trebles; the number of single stitches worked between each increase and decrease can be altered to give wider braids.

186   A firm wide braid made entirely of slip stitch. The work is formed by working the slip stitch one way, ie the yarn is cut at the end of each row. The work is not turned and the yarn is rejoined at the start of each row. When working the slip stitch the hook is placed into the single back loop of each stitch of the previous row. Patterns on this braid can be made by alternating the hook position between the back single

loop and the front single loop for each slip stitch made. One coloured yarn gives the best effect when altering the hook position.

Patterns can also be formed by using different colours which are carried behind the work when not in use. Loops are formed on the wrong side by these yarns. (To avoid loops on the wrong side: hold yarn(s) not in use behind work, place hook into next stitch with yarn(s) not in use lying above hook, follow with another slip stitch in next stitch with yarn(s) not in use lying below hook – the yarn forming the slip stitches will conceal the yarns not in use.) There is a definite right and wrong side to this braid. Figure 186 uses three colours. The braid is known as *Bosnian braid*.

Crochet fringes
See also crochet hairpin fringes in Chapter 14, page 88.

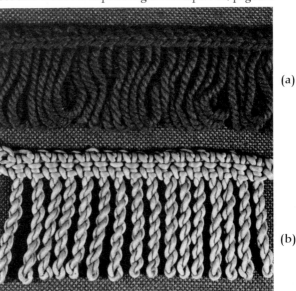

(a)

(b)

187   Two fringes: (a) looped (b) looped and twisted
(a)   Two yarns are used for this fringe. Wrap yarn around a gauge[2] to the full extent of its length.

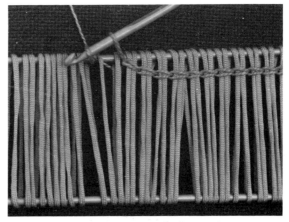

188   With a second yarn, work slip stitches over two loops, ie 4 vertical strands of yarn.

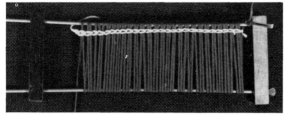

189 One row of slip stitch complete. Slip stitches should lie between loops placed on gauge, to prevent the fringe unravelling.

190 Completed fringe with 3 rows of slip stitch. Secure slip stitch at end of row.

(b) A twisted fringing using one yarn. Make a chain foundation length and work the twisted fringe into this foundation. Insert hook into 2nd chain from hook and work 1 slip stitch. *Extend loop on hook 12 cm. Twist anti-clockwise until the yarn twists back on itself, thus halving the length of the original loop.

191 Insert hook into stitch at base of twist, that is the original chain stitch, yarn over hook and draw yarn through and through loop on hook. Insert hook into next chain stitch, yarn over hook, draw yarn through chain stitch and through loop on hook.* Repeat * to *. It is difficult to make all twisted loops the same length – counting the number of times each loop is twisted should produce loops of equal length.

192 and 193 A very decorative coiled fringing. Make a chain foundation the required depth of the fringe. To form the coiled effect, work 4 trebles into each chain stitch. At the tip of the fringe, double crochet stitches followed by half trebles can be worked to form a more tapered start to the coil. Figure 193 features coiled fringing around the hemline of a striped coat. Patons and Baldwins double knitting yarns in various different shades were selected for this design. 62 × 25 gm balls of Trident DK yarn would be required for this coat.

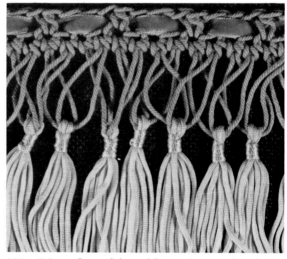

194 Fringe formed by additional yarn placed into

crochet loops. The loops are formed by the method explained in figure 182a, extending the loops to measure 4 cm. When the required length of crochet with loops is complete, insert hook into 2nd stitch below last loop made, yarn over hook and draw through yarn. Work along the crochet just made. 3 chain. *1 chain, miss 1 stitch, 1 treble in next stitch,* repeat from * to * to end of row.

Velvet ribbon is threaded through the spaces formed by the treble stitches. The additional yarn is placed through 2 crochet loops and held in place by a securing yarn (black in diagram). Trim the cut ends. This makes an attractive trimming for lamp shades.

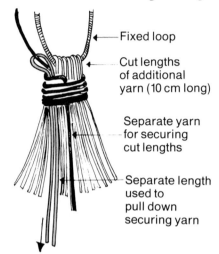

195   Diagram to show the method of attaching and securing the cut lengths of yarn onto a fixed loop. The same method is used for making tassels by increasing the number of cut lengths of yarn used.

Note   When winding the securing yarn (black) attach a 60 cm (approx.) length of yarn at the top of the winding position with an overhand knot and leave a short end hanging freely as shown. Continue to wind the yarn down the winding position, keeping each wrap evenly placed. Return upwards making a double wind to position the final cut end at the top, ready to be secured as shown by the separate length (shaded).

196   A straight braid with additional yarn placed

into chained loops. The braid consists of 1 row in double crochet, 1 row in spaced trebles as explained for figure 194 * to *, followed by 1 row in double crochet. To work the chained loops: 10 chain, slip stitch into 5th chain from hook, 5 chain, leave 3 stitches between working each chained loop. Place additional yarn for tassels as explained above through the loop in the middle of the chain stitches. Trim the cut ends.

Decorative edgings using pompoms and covered polystyrene balls

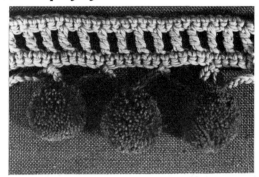

197   Pompoms added to the base braid shown in figure 196. To make a pompom: cut two pieces of card as shown in figure 198 and place yarn round and round the card by threading into the centre. When the centre is almost closed use a bodkin for the final twists. The centre should be quite closed before cutting the yarn around the outer edge of the circle, by placing scissors between the two thicknesses of card. Secure the cut yarn by placing a very strong thread between the card and securing very firmly. Remove card by cutting apart and trim ball. The balls are sewn into the chained loop for this example.

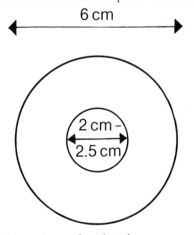

198   Cut two pieces of card to these measurements – the centre hole can vary from 2 cm to 2.5 cm depending on the thickness of the yarn to be used. A thicker yarn requires a larger hole to give a good density to the finished ball. These measurements would produce a ball of approximately 5 cm in diameter.

Yarn pompoms make very useful additional trimmings for tie and belt ends.

199 and 200   Crochet balls feature in both these examples.

Figure 199 uses Russia braid – the balls are placed onto a needlemade triangular edging.

The suggested yarn for making the crochet-covered balls is a tubular rayon cord and a No. 3.00 ISR crochet hook is used. The balls are 4 cm in diameter. Work 2 chain stitch, work 8 double crochet into second chain from hook, ie one round complete. Mark with a safety pin. Work 2 double crochet into next 8 double crochet. Work 1 double crochet into next double crochet for three rounds. Insert ball or cotton wool. Work 1 double crochet over 2 stitches 8 times. Work 1 double crochet in next 8 stitches. Thread yarn through 1 loop of last 8 stitches and pull tightly. Secure yarn and cut leaving enough length to sew onto trimming.

Note   This technique is formed in spirals. For more details see Chapter 13, page 84. Some people may find that they work more or less stitches than those given above, this will depend on the tension, the yarn and hook size, and the size of the ball to be covered. These instructions are given as a guide only.

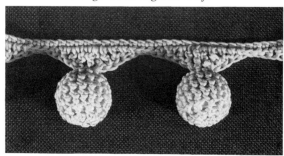

The covered balls in figure 200 are sewn onto a base crochet using a tubular rayon cord and a No. 3.00 ISR crochet hook. Work 1 row in double crochet for required length of trimming. Second row: *1 slip stitch into next 3 stitches, 1 double crochet in next stitch, 1 half treble in next stitch, 1 treble in next stitch, 1 triple treble in next stitch, 1 chain, 1 triple treble in next stitch in first row, 1 double treble stitch in next stitch, 1 treble stitch in next stitch, 1 half treble stitch in next stitch, 1 double crochet in next stitch.* Repeat from * to * to end of trimming.

The covered balls are sewn onto the chain stitches between the triple treble stitches.

6 – Forming crochet fabrics

Crochet can be used in many different ways to form fabrics. This chapter covers some of the more unusual methods, including the use of colour to form patchwork effects, the making and joining of individual motifs, the use of stripes, braids and cords, and crazy or free patchwork. All these techniques can be utilized to suit one's own tastes. All are suitable for adapting to designs for your own garments.

Continuous patchwork

Patchwork is usually thought of as a method of joining together small pieces of fabric in order to make a large piece of fabric. The same principle can be applied to crochet. Small pieces of yarn may be worked together to form a larger area. For continuous patchwork, the crochet stitches follow on using the different colours and no sewing together is required.

When working on a definite project, for example, a garment, designs should be carefully planned with the pattern of the patchwork crochet charted onto squared paper. Two simple charted patterns are shown to illustrate the use of squared paper: the different symbols indicate the different colours to be used.

201 Charted patchwork patterns to illustrate the use of colour. 1 square represents 1 double crochet stitch The best crochet stitch for patchwork is the double crochet – this gives a firm close texture. All yarns selected should be of similar weight for patchwork although yarns of different textures could be used in one fabric piece. The choice of colour is most important and should be thoughtfully planned.

202 A basic squared patchwork. Two colours are used – see figure 201 (a).

203 A basic church window patchwork using many colours – see figure 201 (b).

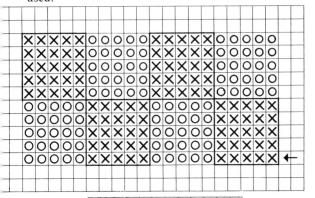

01 (a)

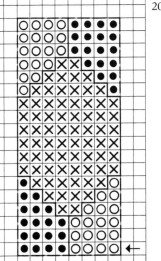

201(b)

204 An irregular patchwork pattern
Note When working patchwork using different coloured yarns, a special technique should be used for the changeover of colour. Figure 205 illustrates this process. At this stage it may be useful to refer back to

figure 48, page 19 showing the working of the double crochet stitch. It will be noted that the two loops forming the 'chain' stitch or top of double crochet stitch for placing the hook on the following row are formed to the *left*-hand side of the working stitch. Therefore the new colour must be placed into the double crochet stitch before the stitch is completed, in order for the top of the double crochet stitch *and* the base of the stitch to be the same colour. This method of introducing a new colour during a working row should always be used.

205 (a)   The first stage of the double crochet stitch has been worked in the darker coloured yarn, and the second colour has completed the stitch. The light coloured yarn will now form the top of the next double crochet stitch.

205 (b)   5 double crochet stitches have been worked in the lighter colour.

Striped patchwork

Interesting fabrics can be simply and easily made by the use of strips. Strips can be worked in different colours using stripes. Each new colour is placed at the start of a new row. Usually two rows are worked in each colour. However, many variations and permutations are possible using two or more colours. Yarns of equal weight are recommended. Double crochet stitch gives the best fabrics.

206   Two strips of crochet worked in stripes form this fabric. The strips are sewn together.

207   Four strips of crochet worked in stripes again, using wider stripes, form this fabric. The diagonal strips form a chevron pattern in the centre. The diagonal lines are worked in two colours, working 4 rows of double crochet in each colour. To start a diagonal strip, begin with 2 chain. Work 2 double crochet into the 2nd chain from hook. Turn work. Work 1 chain, 1 double crochet stitch into 2nd stitch from hook, 1 double crochet into next stitch. 2 double crochet into last stitch. Turn work. Continue in this manner increasing 1 stitch at the beginning and end of each row until one side measures the required strip depth. Continue working in double crochet, changing colours every 4 rows. The diagonal lines are made by increasing 1 stitch at the start of your row, and decreasing 1 stitch at the end of the same row. The shaping is worked on every row. When working increased and decreased stitches in this manner, it is important to keep the single turning chains worked at the start of each row very loose – a curved edge will result if worked too tightly. To end a diagonal strip, decrease 1 stitch at the beginning and end of every row until no stitches are left.

Using this diagonal striped technique, many dramatic patchwork fabrics can be made, altering and changing the width and colour depth of the stripes. For methods of sewing the strips together when completed, please refer to Chapter 17, Working methods.

208   Coat worked in Patons and Baldwins' double knitting yarns. The collar uses the diagonal technique. 46 × 25 gm balls were used for this coat

Patchwork using triangles, squares and circles

Regular shapes such as triangles, squares and circles can all be used to form a crochet fabric. All yarns should be carefully selected and trial motifs worked out before embarking on a project. The shapes should be made and joined together either by sewing or a crochet method – see Chapter 17. The motifs can all be the same size or different sizes of the same shape. However, careful planning is essential. When sufficient shapes are complete, they should be laid onto your garment design and joined.

209   A jacket using patchwork triangles. The garment design is given in Chapter 17. To work the triangles:

Row 1   2 chain. 2 double crochet into 2nd chain from hook. Turn work.

Row 2   1 chain. 1 double crochet into 2nd stitch from hook, ie 1 increased stitch.

1 double crochet in each of the next 2 stitches. Turn work.

Row 3   1 chain. 1 double crochet in 2nd stitch from hook, ie 1 increased stitch. 1 double crochet in each of the next 3 stitches. Turn work. Continue increasing 1 stitch at the start of each row until the triangle is the size you require. The triangles in the jacket measure: 6 cm high, 6 cm base (for the smaller triangle), 11 cm high, 9 cm base (for the larger triangle).

A selection of Patons and Baldwins' *Trident* 4-ply yarns was selected for the design. The triangles are joined together – tip to base, base to tip to form a strip. The strips are then joined together to form the fabric.

Circles of all sizes and colours using any type of crochet stitches form an excellent shape for patchwork. The circles are sewn together at the positions where they touch and small spaces are inevitable. These spaces must be considered when designing a garment.

210   A variety of circles using various Twilley yarns in shades of red and orange. Some circles are plain, some have stitchery in their centres.

To make the circle: wrap yarn around a gauge (eg large wooden knitting needle) 20 times, remove yarn from gauge, and work double crochet directly into the centre hole. The double crochet stitches should be closely and evenly placed around the yarn forming the circle. Secure the end when all the circle is covered. To vary the stitch on the circle, a second row of double crochet is worked from left to right to give a raised stitch effect. Plain weaving and spider's webs[3] decorate the centres of some circles. The thickness of the circles is varied by the number of times the yarn is used to form the initial shape. Use different gauges to make different sized motifs. See figure 413, page 136 and colour plate 7, between pages 92/3.

Like the circle, the square makes a very good basic shape for patchwork. There are many traditional crochet patterns available for making squares. They are simple to join and no spaces are left. The squares should be accurately made in order to achieve a good patchwork fabric (colour plate 2, between pages 92/3).

Colours:

A = Ailsa Blue

B = Skye Mix

C = White

211   Square motif – instructions. The finished garment is shown in colour plate 2, between pages 92/3. With colour B: 4 chain. Join with a slip stitch to the first chain made to form a circle.

Round 1   2 chain to count as 1 half treble. Insert hook into the circle for all stitches of this round. Work

1 half treble, 1 chain, *2 half treble, 1 chain*, 3 times. Join to 3rd chain with a slip stitch.

Round 2 Slip stitch over next 2 stitches. 3 chain to count as 1 treble. Into first 1-chain space work (1 treble, 2 chain, 2 treble) to form corner shaping. *Into the next 1-chain space work (2 treble, 2 chain, 2 treble)*, repeat from * to * 3 times. Join with a slip stitch into 3rd chain at start of round.

Round 3 1 chain to count as 1 double crochet. 1 double crochet in next stitch of previous round. *(1 half treble, 1 treble, 2 chain, 1 treble, 1 half treble) into corner space. 1 double crochet in next 4 stitches*. Repeat from * to * 3 times. (1 half treble, 1 treble, 2 chain, 1 treble, 1 half treble) into next 1-chain space. 1 double crochet into next 2 stitches. Join with a slip stitch into chain at start of round. Break off yarn and secure.

Round 4 Join in colour A onto a corner space. 3 chain to count as 1 treble. (1 treble, 2 chain, 2 treble) into same space. Join in colour C and work 1 treble in next 7 stitches, working over the yarn A. *Using colour A work (2 treble, 2 chain, 2 treble) into corner space. With colour C work 1 treble into next 7 stitches*, repeat from * to * 3 times. Join with a slip stitch to 3rd chain at start of round.

Round 5 With colour A work 3 chain to count as 1 treble. 1 treble into next stitch of previous round. (2 treble, 2 chain, 2 treble) into corner space. 1 treble in next 2 stitches worked in colour A. *With colour C work 1 treble into next 7 stitches worked in colour C. With colour A work 1 treble into next 2 stitches, (2 trebles, 2 chain, 2 trebles) into corner space, 1 treble into next 2 stitches worked in colour A*, repeat from * to * 3 times. With colour C work 1 treble into next 7 stitches worked in colour C. Slip stitch into 3rd chain at start of round. Break off yarn A and leave loop on hook.

Round 6 Join in colour B and work 3 chain to count as 1 treble. 1 treble into next stitch of previous round. *With colour C work 1 treble into next 2 stitches. (2 treble, 2 chain, 2 treble) into corner space. 1 treble into first 2 stitches in colour A. With colour B work 1 treble in next 11 stitches*, repeat from * to * 3 times. With colour C work 1 treble into next 2 stitches, (2 treble, 2 chain, 2 treble) into corner space. 1 treble into first 2 stitches in colour A. With colour B work 1 treble into next 9 stitches. Join with a slip stitch to 3rd chain at start of round. Break off yarns and secure.

Note When changing from one colour to another, use the technique explained at the beginning of this chapter.

When using two colours on the same round, carry the yarn not in use behind your work, and work each crochet stitch over the yarn not in use to conceal and avoid loops.

Continuous strips using chain stitch and different yarns

Interesting strips using yarn types differing in thickness, colour and texture form this fabric. No joining is required and the strips are worked continuously in rows.

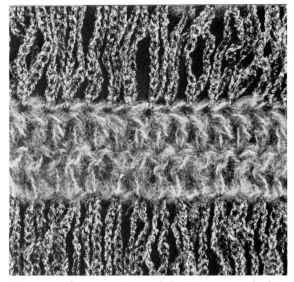

212 A mohair yarn is used for 2 rows worked in treble stitch worked to and fro in the normal way. Break off yarn. The second strip is formed with lengths of 30 chain stitches using a lurex yarn. Each chain length is joined with a slip stitch to the treble stitch of the previous row. Work 1 chained loop for each treble stitch. Break off yarn. The following treble stitch row has to be worked into a slip stitch row worked over the chained loops. To work the slip stitch row: join in the yarn for the treble stitch (mohair in the sample shown) to the first chain loop by placing a slip loop on hook – place hook through chained loop. Draw yarn through loop and through yarn on hook. *Place hook through next chained loop, draw yarn through chained loop and through stitch on hook*, repeat from * to * to end of chained loop row.

213 Lurex yarn and a cotton yarn form this sample.

Work 6 rows in double crochet in the lurex yarn. The chained loop row is formed in the cotton yarn making 40 chain stitches. The slip stitch row which is worked prior to the 6 double crochet rows, illustrates different sequences of combining the chained loops – some are crossed, twisted, woven and knotted. The yarn has to be cut at the end of each completed stripe, in order to be able to work the chained loops from the same side of the fabric each time.

Fabrics formed with cords and braids

Cords and narrow braids can be used to form fabrics. This work used to be referred to as mignardise crochet, and a commercial braid with little loops formed a skeleton for basic crochet stitches.

214   A lace edging using a commercial braid and basic crochet stitches. A pattern should first be drawn out for the braid. The braid is then tacked onto the pattern which can be drawn onto a firm piece of calico or firm brown paper. Crochet, using any of the basic stitches, is then worked to join and secure the braiding. Much practice is required to achieve a satisfactory result which lies quite flat. A good and suitable design is imperative – the lines should be continuous for the braiding and the spaces between the lines of the pattern should be varied but not too large. Curves are possible but sharp points are best avoided. When all the braid is held in place using various crochet stitches, the braid can be removed from the calico base.

The crochet braid illustrated in figure 178, page 47 could be used for this technique. This braid has a loop (not open) on the side through which the crochet hook can pass. Many of the hair pin braids illustrated in Chapter 14 are also suitable.

Jacquard type crochet patterns

Designs can be drawn using jacquard type patterns – that is, crochet patterns using colours worked directly into the crochet fabric. The patterns are worked out on graph paper in a similar manner to the example in the first section of this chapter. Again, double crochet stitch is to be recommended, and usually 1 square represents 1 double crochet stitch. It can, however, be slightly confusing when translating a square on the graph paper to represent 1 stitch because 1 crochet stitch is not exactly square. Therefore some designs can become rather misshaped and widened. Practice will enable you to equate your stitch with the charted design of the graph paper.

215   A simple flower design worked in three colours, using double crochet stitch. The sample is, in fact, a small bag and has been worked in continuous circles – ie one way double crochet. While using the jacquard type crochet, observe the note on page 56.

Crazy Patchwork using different yarns and leather shapes

Crochet stitches may be worked in any direction, either left to right, up and down, round and round, diagonally, as zigzags or elongations etc. To start such a piece of fabric you can use a crochet ring or a piece of leather. The leather can be any shape.

216   Leather pieces, cut in rough ovals forming a starting point. Holes are made around the edges about 4–6 mm inside the cut edge and double crochet is then worked into the holes. It is sometimes difficult to know how many double crochet stitches to work in each hole. To work out how many double crochet

stitches (or whatever other stitch you choose) you
should work, measure along the edge of the leather
using a tape measure on its side, then work a separate
trial piece of crochet using the same stitch and yarn
which is to be used around the leather shape. If, for
example 40 stitches in your trial piece measure 10 cm
wide, and the measurement around the leather shape
is 40 cm, it will be clear that you will have to
work 4 double crochet stitches for every 1 cm on the
leather. Therefore with holes placed 0.5 cm apart, 2
double crochet stitches should be worked into each
hole, 160 stitches in total. This example is given as a
guide, and you will develop methods of working as
you experiment. Be prepared to try out new yarns,
materials and stitches for this type of patchwork.
Also, be prepared to unravel a row or two if your work
does not lie flat. You will find that stitches have to be
decreased at sharp concave angels and increased on
convex angles. Figure 216 illustrates a variety of
stitches and lines of colour and texture. It is a detailed
photograph of the bolero shown in the colour plate 4,
between pages 92/3. The shape of the outline for the
design of this bolero is given in Chapter 17, page 117. It
is impossible to give written instructions for designs of
this type and it is up to the individual to work out her
own ideas.

7 – Filet crochet

Many crochet techniques produce fabrics which are similar in appearance to fabrics produced by other well established methods of working; filet crochet is such a technique. In appearance filet crochet resembles *guipure d'art* which is also known as *filet brodé* and *filet guipure* – a modern revival of the *opus filatorium* or darned netting used in the fourteenth century.[4] Filet is the French for net which gives the name – filet crochet.

A squared 'net' mesh forms the base fabric which is made first, using the traditional netting technique. Embroidered decoration is then applied to form various naturalistic or geometric designs. The decorative work applied to the net consists of various embroidery stitches such as buttonhole, and a wide range and variation of darning stitches. Crochet filet work produces a similar fabric by working both processes, ie the making of the net and the 'filling in' darning stitch patterns, simultaneously.

Today, filet crochet is most often found on old domestic linen, such as table cloths and bed linen. Some personal articles of clothing used filet crochet trimmings. Filet crochet was very popular during the later part of the Victorian period and during the Edwardian decade and most examples seen today were probably made during this time.

In crochet, the net background is made by using two types of stitch only – the chain and the treble. The square of the net is made by working 1 treble, 2 chain – missing 2 stitches of the previous row – followed by 1 treble. This is called a *space*. This last treble forms the first treble of the next space. Therefore, a space covers 3 stitches.

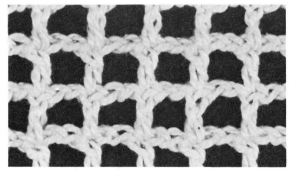

217   A crochet net mesh. To form a pattern on the net mesh, the spaces are filled in with 2 treble stitches. This is called a *block*. Thus, one block consists of 2 trebles, with 1 treble on either side which follow through the mesh grid. A block, like a space, covers 3 stitches. There are various modifications found in some old pieces of filet crochet. The treble stitch is sometimes worked with an extra twist, ie yarn over hook, insert hook into next stitch, yarn over hook and draw through yarn. Yarn over hook and draw through 1 loop (yarn over hook and draw through 2 loops) twice. Treble stitches worked in this way produce a more ridged effect to the blocks. Patterns can be worked out on graph paper, hatching out the squares to form the pattern. The hatched squares are worked in treble stitch to form a block, the squares left unmarked are worked in chain stitches – a space. Before working out a pattern, it is important to work a trial sample to test the shape of the mesh. The squares of the mesh should be square, ie the chain stitches and the treble stitch should be the same length. If not, your design will be distorted in shape. If your mesh does not work out quite square, try another sample using a different hook size and gauging the length of your treble stitch to equal the length of the chain stitches forming the spaces. The following instructions are given as an introduction to the basic principles of filet crochet. Coats mercer crochet thread makes the best yarn for this type of work. Using these samples as a starting point, try the techniques using different yarns – perhaps thicker and coarser with a larger hook size. Experiment with the additional embroidery stitches on the basic net mesh. Try contrasting colours and ribbons for weaving through the spaces.

Some technical difficulties which can occur when working filet crochet

1   To calculate the number of chain stitches for the foundation: a length of chain stitches for the foundation should be calculated as a multiple of $3 + 1$.

2   Starting a row with a block: work 3 chain to count as 1 treble, work 1 treble into 5th stitch from hook. 1 treble into next 2 stitches.

3   Starting a row with a space: work 5 chain to count as 1 treble and 1 space. Work 1 treble into 9th stitch from hook.

4   The last treble: at the end of each row, care should be taken always to place the last treble stitch into the correct position in order to have a vertical line of treble stitches along the edges of your work.

5   Placing the hook into the chain stitches: when working treble stitches over a space, the hook may be inserted into the chain stitches or over the chain stitches, that is, placing the hook into the space itself. In figure 218 the treble is made by inserting the hook *into* the chain stitch which will give a firmer and well formed fabric. It is sometimes more difficult to do this, and more time consuming. However, most examples use the second method which is easier and quicker.

6   When the lace is complete: careful blocking by pinning and pressing is essential, see Chapter 17, page 119. Sometimes the fabric requires starching.

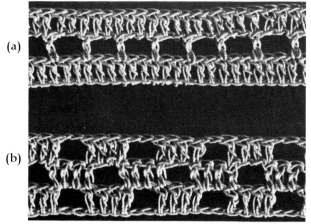

(a)

(b)

218   Two small braids to illustrate the use of blocks
and spaces.
Example (a)   Three rows form the braid.
   Row 1 – all blocks.
   Row 2 – all spaces.
   Row 3 – all blocks.
Example (b)   Three rows form the braid.
   Row 1 – *1 block, 1 space* repeated.
   Row 2 – *1 space, 1 block* repeated.
   Row 3 – *1 block, 1 space* repeated.

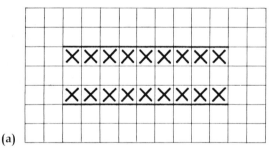

(a)

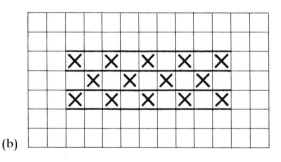

(b)

220   An under bodice top, made during the 1880s
using cotton yarn. It is very typical of the filet crochet
work of this period. The convolvulus pattern is
clearly shown by the placing of the blocks.

221   A page from a crochet worker's sample book
showing many different patterns – some of the
examples are seen in filet crochet work.
Two other patterns which occur in filet crochet are the
lacet and a 'spider shape' pattern.

✗   Represents 1 block

☐   Represents 1 space

219   Charted filet crochet patterns for the illustrations in figure 218

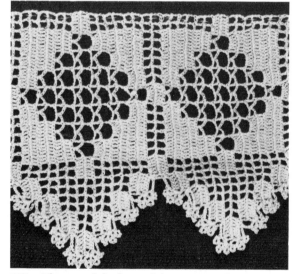

222   The use of the lacet. A lacet covers 2 squares on
the net mesh. This consists of 2 diagonal lines forming
a V shape over 2 squares. To work the V: work 3 chain,
miss 2 stitches, 1 double crochet into the next stitch, 3
chain, miss 2 stitches, 1 treble in next stitch. On the

return row, work 5 chain, with 1 treble on either side – that is 1 treble into each treble opposite the diagonal line.

223 The use of the 'spider's shape' pattern. The following instructions explain the making of this pattern – it forms part of the whole pattern of the filet crochet edging, but the instructions cover this particular shape only, ie 28 stitches.

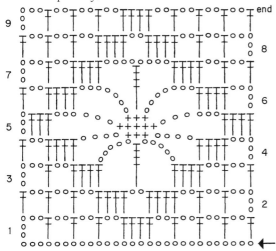

224 Diagram of the 'spider's shape' pattern. Please refer to the chart on page 34 for the symbols used in crochet.

This design is worked over 9 rows and 28 stitches. Work 28 chain.

Row 1 5 chain to count as 1 treble and 2 chain for the space.
1 treble into 9th chain from hook. (2 chain, miss 2 stitches, 1 treble in next stitch) 3 times. 1 treble in next 3 stitches. (2 chain, miss 2 stitches, 1 treble in next stitch) 4 times. Turn work.
Row 2 5 chain to count as 1 treble and 2 chain for the space.
1 treble in 9th stitch from hook. (2 chain, miss 2 stitches, 1 treble in next stitch) twice. 1 treble in next 3 stitches, 2 chain, miss 2 stitches, 1 treble in next 4 stitches. (2 chain, miss 2 stitches, 1 treble in next stitch) 3 times. Turn work.
Row 3 5 chain to count as 1 treble and 2 chain for the space.
1 treble in 9th stitch from hook. 2 chain, miss 2

stitches. 1 treble in next 4 stitches. 5 chain, 1 triple treble in next space. 5 chain. 1 treble in last treble stitch of next block. 1 treble in next 3 stitches. (2 chain, miss 2 stitches, 1 treble in next stitch) twice. Turn work.
Row 4 5 chain to count as 1 treble and 2 chain for the space.
1 treble in 9th stitch from hook. 1 treble in next 3 stitches. 4 chain, miss 7 stitches, 1 double crochet into next 3 stitches. 4 chain, miss 7 stitches, 1 treble in next 4 stitches. 2 chain, miss 2 stitches, 1 treble in next stitch. Turn work.
Row 5 3 chain to count as 1 treble. 1 treble in 5th stitch from hook. 1 treble in next 2 stitches. 6 chain, miss 6 stitches, 1 double crochet into next 5 stitches, 6 chain, miss 6 stitches, 1 treble in next 4 stitches. Turn work.
Row 6 5 chain to count as 1 treble and 2 chain for the space. 1 treble in 9th stitch from hook. 1 treble in next 3 stitches. 7 chain, miss 4 stitches, 1 double crochet in next 3 stitches, 7 chain, miss 4 stitches, 1 treble in next 4 stitches, 2 chain, miss 2 stitches, 1 treble in next stitch. Turn work.
Row 7 5 chain to count as 1 treble and 2 chain for the space. 1 treble in 9th stitch from hook. 2 chain, miss 2 stitches, 1 treble in next stitch. 1 treble in next 3 stitches, 4 chain, miss 5 stitches, 1 triple treble in next stitch. 4 chain, miss 5 stitches, 1 treble in next 4 stitches. (2 chain, miss 2 stitches, 1 treble in next stitch) twice. Turn work.
Row 8 5 chain to count as 1 treble and 2 chain for the space. 1 treble in 9th stitch from hook. (2 chain, miss 2 stitches, 1 treble in next stitch) twice. 1 treble in next 3 stitches, 2 chain, miss 3 stitches, 1 treble in next 4 stitches. (2 chain, miss 2 stitches, 1 treble in next stitch) 3 times. Turn work.
Row 9 Repeat row 1.
When filet crochet is used as an edging, the crochet is worked with one straight edge for sewing onto the fabric of the article to be trimmed. The other edge is usually pointed. This will involve the technique of increasing and decreasing. For a trimming for a square article, the filet crochet edging has to be mitred – a right angled corner worked in the process of making the crochet trimming. Again, increasing and decreasing of the squares is involved. The straight edge can be made by the foundation chain, as shown in figure 218. However, for trimmings requiring a pointed outer edge, the side edge of the crochet forms the sewing on edge as shown in figures 222 and 223.

The method of working a pointed edge to the filet crochet trimming

The design can be worked out on graph paper to give a stepped or pointed pattern.
To increase a square at the start of a row To increase a block, work 6 chain, 1 treble into 5th stitch from hook, 1 treble in next 2 stitches. If more than 1 block increase is required at the start of a row, add 3 chain for each additional block required.

To increase a space, work 8 chain, 1 treble in 9th chain from hook. If more than 1 space increase is required at the start of a row, add 3 chain for each additional space required.

To increase a square at the end of a row   To increase a block, extra chain stitches must be worked at the beginning of the previous row to allow for an extension to remain at the end of the row requiring the increase. At the beginning of the preceeding row requiring the increase, work 6 chain, miss 1 chain, slip stitch over the next 3 chain leaving 2 chain stitches unworked. Allow these 2 stitches to lie upright and count as 1 treble for the current row being worked. Continue along this row, following the pattern. On the return row, work in pattern to the last 3 slip stitches and work 1 treble in next 3 stitches.

To increase a space, work the chain extension on the previous row as above, and work the space increase by working 2 chain, miss 2 stitches, 1 treble in last slip stitch.

For each additional increased square (either block or space), add 3 additional chain stitches to the chained extension of the previous row requiring the increase. The number of slip stitches will be increased accordingly on the return row.

To decrease a square at the start of a row. The same method applies for blocks and spaces. Miss first stitch of row and slip stitch over the next 3 stitches. Then continue in the normal way. For each additional square decreased, slip stitch over a further 3 stitches for each square.

To decrease a square at the end of a row: The same method applies for blocks and spaces. Work to the position of the last block or space, turn work and start the next row in the normal way.

Many filet crochet trimmings worked with a shaped edge have a further row of crochet stitches worked in a continuous line all around the shaped edge. This additional trimming is worked when all the main part is completed. Double crochet stitch makes a good final row. 3 stitches are worked into each side of each square.

225   An edging worked onto the completed trim using several different stitches to form a picot edge.

Working corners in filet crochet

There are two methods: (a)   a mitred corner where the crochet is worked in steps (method 1); (b)   a corner cut straight (method 2).
226   Graph design for working a filet corner. Each square represents: 1 block, or 1 space per row

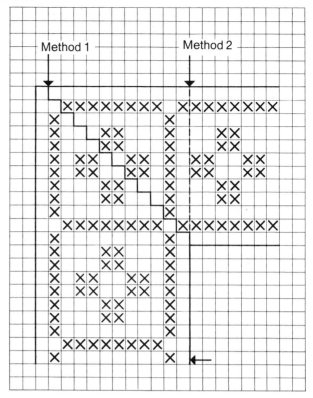

In both examples the direction of the crochet changes. For both methods it is essential for your crochet to form true squares, because each treble stitch and each chain space has to be worked in both directions at the corner and must be the same length.

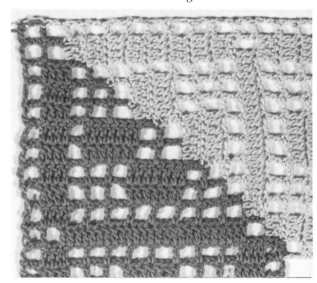

227   A corner worked in two colours to illustrate the stepped line. The dark colour is worked first, and the lighter shade is joined to the outer point of the corner. The dark shade, worked in the horizontal direction in the illustration, decreases 1 square (block or space) on each row until 1 square remains. The lighter

shade which is worked in the vertical direction in the illustration is joined onto the outer point, ie the corner of the last square made. 1 increased square has to be made on every row to fit in with the darker shade working the decrease. The diagonal edge of each square worked in the darker shade forms the outer edge of each square to be made in the lighter shade.

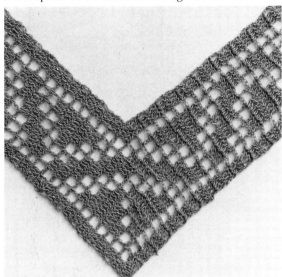

228 A simple corner designed and worked to illustrate this method of turning corners. When worked in the same colour it is difficult to see the difference in the direction of the rows. This is usually found to be the most satisfactory method of working a corner, but some people find this 'stepping' method rather difficult.

An easier method is shown in figure 226 method 2. The corner finishes with a straight line in the vertical direction, (dotted line) and when changing to the horizontal direction the crochet is simply joined onto the straight edge.

For both examples of turning corners, a careful and detailed graph pattern should be followed in order for the blocks and spaces to be worked in their correct positions.

8 – Crochet worked over cords

Double crochet is a very versatile stitch. It is used very successfully in its own right to form a fabric, and the stitch can also be worked with the addition of a secondary yarn. The secondary yarn can be placed into the double crochet stitch so as to give interesting and exciting textures.

Crochet worked over cords is such a technique. Any cord or yarn may be used, depending on the result required and the purpose for which the fabric is to be used. The technique is used much in Irish crochet lace (see Chapter 18) and forms a raised outline to many designs.

The stitch used for this technique is usually the double crochet stitch, although other stitches can be used. The method of working over a cord is simple and produces a very firm fabric which resists stretching. The cord introduced with the double crochet stitch may be string, piping cord, braids, fancy yarns used singly or in groups. Depending on the materials and yarns selected, the fabric produced may be used for bags, belts, shoe and sandle soles, household articles such as rugs, wall hangings, baskets and place mats. There are three examples of introducing the cord:

(a) Working double crochet onto a foundation chain length.
(b) Working double crochet with *no* foundation chain length.
(c) Working double crochet directly onto an existing fabric.

Example (a)   Work a chain length for the foundation. Apply the cord by placing along the chain length. Work into each chain stitch in the normal way, placing the hook into the foundation chain so that the cord lies over the hook; as you draw the yarn through the chain foundation and complete the double crochet stitch, it will be seen that the yarn is caught behind the cord, thus enclosing the cord in the middle of the double crochet stitch. Continue working in double crochet into each chain stitch to end of row. It will be noted that for each double crochet stitch there will be two vertical strands of yarn on both the back and the front of the cord (see figure 229). The cord is not always completely covered, so the colour of the cord must be taken into account before starting a project. Cords can be dyed to match the main colour in order to prevent the cord showing through the crochet. At the end of the row, the cord is turned as you turn the crochet work in the normal way; the cord will form a loop and should be placed along the top of the double crochet row just completed. Work another double crochet row into the preceeding row with the cord lying in the centre of each double crochet stitch. Sometimes it may be necessary to adjust the double crochet stitches evenly by very slightly pulling the cord.

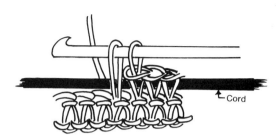

229   Diagram to show the working of double crochet stitch over cord and onto an existing row of double crochet or a foundation chain length

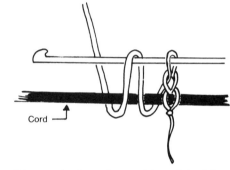

230   Diagram to show the working of double crochet stitch over a cord

Example (b)   Double crochet stitch may be worked directly over a cord with *no* foundation chain. Several pieces of yarn may be substituted for a single cord. Make a slip loop on the hook, and place cord behind hook. With the yarn running below the cord, work 2 chain. The cord should be anchored in the first chain stitch worked. *Place hook in front of cord, and place yarn over hook and draw up in front of cord (230), yarn over hook placing hook over top of cord and draw yarn through both loops on hoop.* Repeat from * to * to end of length. See bag ties in figure 239.

231   A fabric worked in double crochet over cord (eg piping cord No. 5). Several different coloured yarns are used and the yarn and cord were cut at the end of each row to form a one way crochet fabric. The work was not turned at the end of each row.

232 Crochet fabric worked with a 1 cm wide braid in place of a cord. The double crochet is worked in the normal manner, ie 1 row in double crochet, turn work, and work the braid row: place braid along the top edge of the previous row, work 1 chain to count as 1 double crochet and extend the stitch to the same depth as the braid. 1 chain. *Place hook in front of braid and work 1 double crochet in next stitch, placing braid in centre of double crochet stitch, 1 chain, miss 1 stitch*, repeat from * to * to end of row. Turn work and follow with a plain row of double crochet. The braid is cut at the end of each row where applied.

Example (c) Double crochet may be worked over cord(s) working directly onto an existing fabric. Sometimes it is necessary to make a firm edge to an existing shape. The jacket in figure 363 employs this technique. Not only does the cord provide a decorative edge, but it also gives a firm line which will neither drop nor stretch during wear.

To work double crochet onto an existing fabric: the hook may be placed into an existing stitch in the normal manner or it may have to be placed into the vertical side of some stitches. This is not always easy to do. The hook should always be inserted under 2 loops of a vertical side in order to give a neat line. It is, however, difficult, to estimate how many double crochet stitches to work if applying the edging onto a vertical line of treble stitches. A method of working out the number of stitches required is to calculate the amount by working a trial piece of crochet; use the same stitch and yarn and count the number of double crochet stitches worked over a set measurement – for example, say 6 double crochet stitches measure 5 cm. Mark the edge of the crochet fabric, using safety pins or short lengths of coloured yarn at 5 cm intervals. Work 6 double crochet over the cord between each marker. The cord is placed along the edge and the double crochet stitches are worked over the cord as already explained. The cord should be several thicknesses of the *same* yarn in order to match the main fabric yarn. The double crochet stitches may be adjusted along the cord to give a controlled edge to the garment. When working onto a normal row, the double crochet can be worked into each stitch of the fabric so long as the tension and stitch type are equal to the double crochet edging. If there is a difference between the two rows, use the calculated method just explained.

Various sculptured and three-dimensional effects may be achieved by using this technique and substituting fine wire in place of the cord. The petals on the flowers and leaves shown in figure 330 page 97 demonstrate the use of wire. The crochet is moulded to form a 'cupped' shape to the petals.

To work a looped fabric – using fancy yarns in place of a cord

Work in double crochet stitch, using a fancy yarn in place of the cord. The fancy yarn is usually placed in groups of 6–8 thicknesses if the single thickness is rather thin. One, 3 or 5 rows of double crochet without working over the fancy yarns separate the looped rows. To work the row to include the fancy yarn: work over the fancy yarn for all the double crochet stitches on this row. When a loop is required, extend the fancy yarn between 2 double crochet stitches by using a gauge before working the second stitch. A small tube from a ball of cotton makes a good gauge, and some people may simply guess and use the second finger of the right hand. The looped row is worked with the wrong side of the crochet fabric towards you. Work a set number of double crochet stitches before working the next loop, working over the fancy yarn as before. The number of double crochet stitches to be worked between each loop may be regular or varied to produce a surface pattern. The double crochet is worked over the fancy yarns only on the rows requiring the loops. Many variations are possible using this technique.

233 This sample incorporates a single fancy yarn which is very thick and chunky, to form the loops at irregular intervals on every 6th row.

To work a more rounded loop use the following technique. Work over the fancy yarns until the position for the loops is reached. Using the gauge or the second finger of your right hand, form a complete looped circle of the fancy yarn(s) and lay along the back of your row. Work your next stitch placing the hook through the stitch of the previous row and the circle formed. 1 or more double crochet stitches may be placed into this circle. Continue along the row forming loops as required. Work rows of double crochet without the fancy yarns between the looped rows.

234   A fabric using a fancy yarn in several thicknesses to form the loops at irregular intervals on every 6th row. 1 double crochet stitch is worked over the fancy yarns formed into the circle.

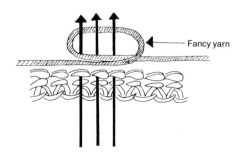

235   A fabric incorporating 6 strands of looped yarn to form loops at regular intervals on every other row. 3 double crochet stitches are worked over the fancy yarns formed into the circle.

Fancy yarn

236   Diagram to show the method of working for figure 235. The yarn is looped behind work. Arrows indicate the position for working double crochet

Crochet over very thick cords suitable for floor coverings

237   A very tough crochet fabric worked in double crochet using a thick nylon cord. Spaced treble stitches have been worked on either side of the nylon cord. A strong string of natural or man-made fibres would make a suitable material for working the double crochet over the nylon – a suitable fabric for floor coverings.

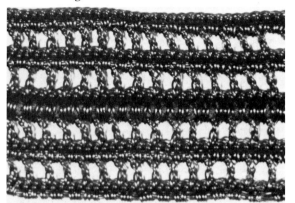

Crochet over cord to form circles

238   Double crochet worked over cord in the form of a circle. This is a useful additional technique and forms a firm circular base for round bags; when worked in oblongs the fabric is suitable for the soles of house boots and shoes.

Method of working in circles: work 12 double crochet directly over the cord (a piping cord No. 5.00 is suitable for a double knitting type yarn); twist cord round to form a circle and adjust the double crochet stitches to lie evenly along the cord. Work 1 slip stitch into the first double crochet worked. Place a safety pin into this stitch to mark the beginning of a new round. Continue to work over the cord, work 2 double crochet into each double crochet of the first round, adjust cord and move safety pin to last stitch made. Continue to work over the cord in continuous rounds, work *2 double crochet into next double crochet, 1 double crochet in next double crochet*, repeat from * to * to end of round, ie safety pin. Adjust cord and move safety pin to stitch just worked. Continue in rounds, increasing by 1 stitch the number of single double crochet stitches worked between each increase on each new round. Move the safety pin to mark the end of each round before starting a new round.

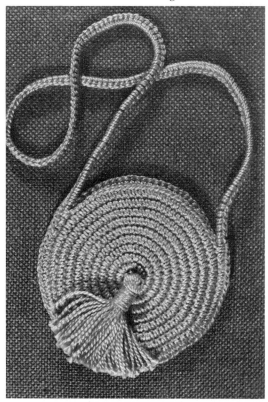

239 A small bag made in Twilley's *Stalite* cotton yarn. Two circles are made and joined together for two-thirds of their circumference. Double crochet is worked over cord to form the hanging strings and is attached round the bag.

9 – Crochet on canvas

Crochet is normally worked to form a fabric without the use of a secondary fabric. In this chapter the introduction of a secondary fabric is illustrated, the secondary fabric used being an embroidery canvas or rug canvas. Depending on the size of the holes in the canvas, select a hook size which will pass through the holes – this will govern the type of yarn to use with the canvas. The technique is based on tambour embroidery, which is a chain stitch surface decoration worked onto a fabric. The fabric should be very taut, ie an embroidery frame or ring should be used. A special tambour hook is required which is extremely fine; it has a sharp point at the hook end to enable the hook to enter through the fabric in order to work a chain stitch.

For the examples shown here, an ordinary crochet hook is used. If using a rug canvas with 3 holes to a square of 2.5 cm, a No. 3.50 ISR crochet hook would be suitable. The yarn chosen should be well and tightly twisted to avoid splitting while working. This type of work lends itself to articles taking much wear and tear, such as bags, stool covers and chair seats and cushions.

Rug canvas is fairly stiff and a frame is not really necessary. To work the crochet over the canvas, first make a slip loop, remove hook and place yarn under the canvas – this will be the wrong side of your work. Place hook on the right side, and insert it into 1 hole of the canvas. Place the slip loop on the hook and draw through the canvas.

place hook into next hole above the last stitch, place yarn over hook and draw yarn through the canvas and through the stitch on the hook. 1 surface chain stitch has been worked over the canvas. Repeat the surface chain stitch for the required pattern.

When working this technique for the first time, you will find it easiest to begin at the base of the canvas and work upwards. You may find it difficult to control the hook through the canvas and to bring the yarn through each time. It is helpful to twist the hook during the process of working a surface chain stitch, ie the barb of the hook should face the direction of the chain line when being inserted; then place the yarn round the hook and turn the hook so that the barb is now facing in the direction of the last chain stitch made. It may also be necessary to experiment with different hook sizes and yarns before you are satisfied with the results. The yarn should always cover the canvas with even and well formed chain stitches.

Surface double crochet stitch may also be worked directly onto canvas. Its appearance is similar to surface chain stitch but the stitch stands higher and above the canvas. To work surface double crochet stitch on canvas: hold the canvas in the same way as for working surface chain stitch. Place hook through 1 hole and attach the slip loop through canvas. Insert hook into *same* hole as last stitch, place yarn round hook and draw through yarn, insert hook into next hole up, yarn round hook and draw yarn through canvas and through both loops on hook – 1 surface double crochet stitch complete. Continue working in surface double crochet stitch to form your line.

It will be seen that the chain stitch may be worked by altering the placement of the hook. The chained lines can be worked vertically, horizontally or diagonally. The hook may be placed into every adjacent hole, or holes may be missed. All designs can be marked onto the canvas with a waterproof felt pen or the pattern can be worked out on graph paper allowing each square to represent one hook insertion. Avoid a tight tension – if the surface stitches are pulled too tightly the canvas base will not lie flat and a puckered fabric will result.

240 and 241   Hold the yarn in the normal way, and

242   A square pattern worked onto canvas using different yarn types and surface chain stitches

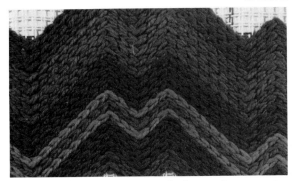

243 A zigzag line pattern worked onto the canvas by placing the surface chain stitches on the diagonal holes of the canvas

The surface double crochet stitch can be modified to give a different stitch texture.

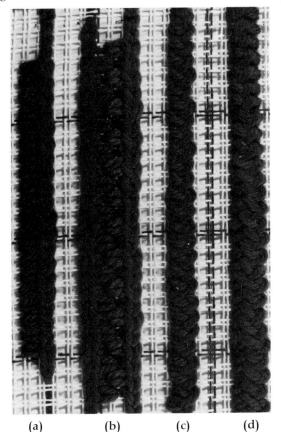

(a)　　　　(b)　　　　(c)　　　　(d)

244 Four stitch variations. The main feature for all the examples is the extending of the loop from the canvas to give width to the surface stitches. Care is required to obtain the correct stitch length each time in order for the yarn to lie over the canvas.
(a) Hold the canvas with the yarn below and the hook above and attach yarn with a slip loop through the canvas. As this stitch is approximately 1.5 cm wide (depending on the canvas type) your design lines will be marked by 2 lines side by side. Work in an upward direction inserting the hook on the right-hand

line of the 2 marked lines. Draw the slip loop through the canvas. *Insert hook into left side of design, 1 hole up, place yarn round hook and draw yarn through canvas and extend the loop to the hole above the last stitch worked (2 loops on hook). Insert hook in next hole on the right-hand side, yarn round hook and draw yarn through both loops on hook – 1 extended surface double crochet stitch has been worked*. Repeat from * to * for required length of design. These instructions are given as a guide, and different spaces can be worked between each stitch to alter the width.
(b) A variation of (a). Two rows of extended surface double crochet stitches worked to dovetail together. Two different stitch lengths form the dovetailing.
(c) and (d) A twisted surface chain stitch. This stitch can vary between 1 cm and 3 cm wide. Again, the design will be indicated by 2 lines. Work as for the surface chain stitches, inserting the hook into adjacent holes, first on the line on the right-hand side, then the line on the left side. Each time the loop on the hook has to be extended to lie in place in the middle of the 2 lines. Some practice is necessary for this twisted surface chain stitch. The 2 examples show different stitch widths. (c) is 1 cm wide – the surface chain stitches are worked from side to side with no space between each line. (d) is 2 cm wide – the surface chain stitches are worked from side to side with 1 hole left as a space between each line. This is referred to as a twisted surface chain stitch.

Crochet on canvas using beads

Beads can be very easily introduced into crochet canvas work. Select a large holed wooden bead and place onto the yarn with which the crochet will be worked. If the beads are loose, ie not on a thread when purchased, use a small needle, or a beading needle for very small beads, and thread all the beads onto a strong thin thread such as nylon. To transfer the beads onto your working yarn use either of the methods shown in figures 245 and 246. When placing the beads onto the canvas, the crochet stitches must be worked from the *wrong side* of the canvas; therefore the chain stitches will be visible from the wrong side only. Hold the canvas, hook and yarn as explained, so that the yarn with the beads is on the under side of the canvas (this will be the right side of the work), and the wrong side of canvas will be facing upwards. The design for the chain stitch may be drawn onto the wrong side of the canvas. Work the chain stitch to attach the beads as follows: place hook through canvas and attach slip loop over hook. Work 1 surface chain stitch, *with the left hand, place 1 bead along the canvas next to last stitch worked, insert hook in a hole above the bead, yarn round hook and draw yarn through canvas and through loop already on hook*, repeat from * to * for required length of design. Depending on the size of the beads being used, the size of the chain stitch appearing on the wrong side of the canvas will have to be adjusted. One or more beads can be placed for each chain stitch worked. Long loops of beads can cause practical problems, but may have a place on a decorative hanging.

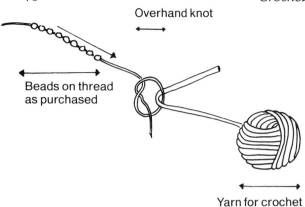

Overhand knot

Beads on thread
as purchased

Yarn for crochet

245   Diagram to illustrate the transfer of beads from a
fine thread, as purchased, to a thicker yarn for the
crochet required

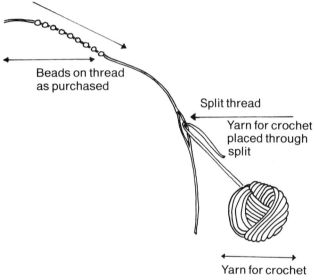

Beads on thread
as purchased

Split thread

Yarn for crochet
placed through
split

Yarn for crochet

246   Diagram to illustrate the transfer of beads from
one thread to another. This method is especially useful
when working with very small beads

247   Long wooden beads used with the modified
surface stitches already explained.

Crochet on canvas for floor rugs

The use of canvas with crochet techniques is an easy
and quick method of making floor coverings. Rug
wools and string are recommended for this technique.
Strips of fabric can also be used, but avoid fabrics
which fray badly.

Surface chain stitch when worked over a thick cord
placed along the canvas, produces a firm fabric of
depth. A thick string or cord, approximately 4–6 mm
in diameter is placed horizontally over the canvas at
regular intervals. Work the surface chain stitch in an
upward direction, working from the right side of the
canvas, crossing the cord at right angles. 1 surface
chain stitch is worked into each adjacent hole securing
1 length of cord for each chain stitch. Repeat the
process by working another row of surface chain
stitches over each line of cord. On both edges of the
canvas, the cord can be extended to form a fringed
edging, and a 4 cm allowance should be left unworked
for turning under to the wrong side. The raw edge of
the canvas can be further neatened by the addition of
a tape bind.

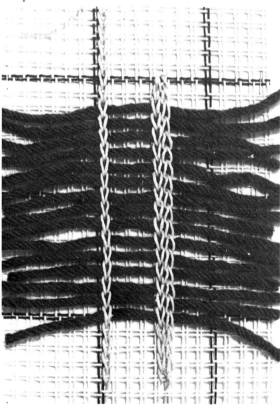

248   The technique used for working crochet on
canvas. String is used for the surface chain stitches;
rug wool for the cord between the canvas and the
chain stitches
249   The same technique modified to produce a piled
fabric. Lay rug wool in place of the cord over the
canvas on the right side. Work a line of surface chain
stitches using string. Place a gauge of 3 cm depth (eg a
ruler) under the rug wool before working a second line

of surface chain stitches next to the first line – the gauge should be placed on its side as shown in the illustration. When the row is complete, remove the gauge and the loops will remain. Work further rows of chain stitches placing the gauge under the rug wool before working the next row of chain stitches.

This technique of producing a pile surface on canvas is a very useful additional method of work, and could be applied to finer canvases using thinner yarns. The fabrics produced using finer materials would have their place in the making of decorative wall hangings, accessories and fashion garments. The looped pile could also be cut and trimmed to give a cut pile effect. The cut lengths could either be equal or different, to give an even more textured effect.

10 – Crochet on net

It is important to read the previous chapter before beginning this one as many of the techniques will be referred to again for working on net. Crochet on net is a further use of the crochet technique applied to a secondary fabric – the fabric forming the base structure for the crochet. This type of work using net as the base fabric used to be known as tambour work on net, and it was very popular during the last century. A small tambour hook produces a chain stitch on the net, the linear design of the chain stitches following the older examples of needlerun net. Sometimes chain stitches were produced by chain stitch sewing machines. Many examples of tambour work on net may still be seen today.

Many of the skills mastered while working on canvas apply to crochet on net. Net is much finer than the canvas used for the techniques in preceeding chapter. There are a number of different fabrics available with a holed mesh, including a variety of dress weight nets. The position of the holes in some nets is different from the holes in canvas; the holes in net run diagonally, in canvas vertically and horizontally. The holes in net give scope for a more varied working line for the surface stitches than in canvas; being finer the lines of the design can be more curved and detailed.

Most nets require an embroidery frame for holding the fabric taut. It is not possible to work a satisfactory design on net held loosely in the hand. It is also important to work your chain stitches so that each stitch is the correct length of the net to be covered below each stitch, and some loosening of the stitches may be required during the process of working. The chain stitches can be worked into every adjacent hole or some holes can be missed. If the embroidery chain stitches are worked too tightly, puckering of the fabric will result.

Crochet on net makes an attractive decoration for wedding veils. Also sections or insertions of net with surface crochet can be introduced to many fashion garments. The coarser nets could have a place in three-dimensional work and wall hangings.

For working surface crochet on a dress weight net, use a fine hook such as a 0.75 ISR and a Coats mercer crochet yarn No. 60 or 80 depending on the size of the holes in the net. For very fine work, sewing threads may be used. The pattern for the net stitches should be drawn up freely and the lines should be continuous and the design linear in style. When the net is placed over the drawing, the outline can be marked onto the net using a white pencil or fabric marker (water erasable).

250 A lightweight net placed in an embroidery ring with a trial run of surface chain stitches to show the various directions possible

251 Part of a white net wedding veil showing the working of a linear design

The application of beads

As explained in the previous chapter, beads can be applied while working surface chain stitches onto a base fabric. To work beads onto a net base, first place the beads onto the working yarn before starting to crochet. Place the fabric into a frame and transfer the design for the beads onto the net. Work the design with the wrong side of the fabric uppermost. As the chain stitches are worked, 1 bead is attached onto the underside of the fabric, which is the right side.

252 4 chain stitches worked on the wrong side,

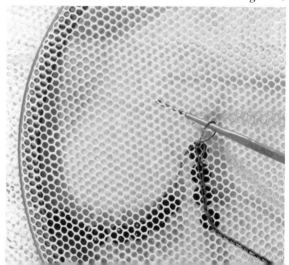

with 4 beads held in place on the right side. The loop on the hook is extended to equal the width of the bead, the hook is inserted along the line of the design and several holes in the net can be missed. One bead should be placed against the net, next to the last stitch worked before drawing the yarn through the net for the next stitch.

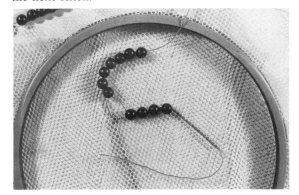

253 The underside of the frame which shows the right side of the fabric and the beads in place

Further embroidery applications to net
When the basic surface chain stitch has been mastered further decorative techniques can be used on net such as cut-out areas, filled-in areas, padded areas and shadow work. All these techniques are best worked with the fabric in a frame with the right side uppermost.

Cut-out areas
Various shapes can be cut away in net and the cut edges neatened with crochet. The holes should not be too large if no further work is to be applied inside the space. Larger holes can be filled in with additional crochet stitches.

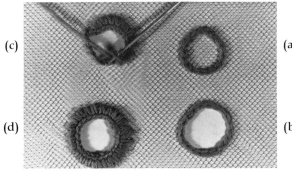

254 The stages of working a simple cut out shape in net.
  (a) Outline the shape with surface chain stitches.
  (b) Cut net away inside the chain stitches.
  (c) Work an extended double crochet stitch over the chain stitch.
  (d) Completed shape.
255 Part of the fabric used in a dancing dress worn by Moslem women in Kuwait showing much surface chain stitch crochet. Circles and ovals have been cut

away and additional crochet applied to fill in these areas. The fabric is a lightweight green voile and the chain stitches are worked in gold threads. Sequins and glass beads also form part of the decoration.

Filled-in areas
Various shapes can be further emphasized by filling in the area with adjacent chain stitches.

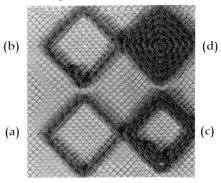

256 The stages of working a simple filled-in shape.
  (a) Outline the shape with surface chain stitches.
  (b) and (c) Continue working in surface chain stitches placing the lines of stitches close together.
  (d) Completed shape.

Padded areas or shadow work
To add colour to a design various shapes can be applied to net using contrasting fabrics. A second piece of transparent fabric such as net is tacked onto the net being used. Outline the shape to be worked in surface chain stitches working over both layers of fabric. When the shape is complete, secure the end of the chain stitches and, using a bodkin and coloured yarn, thread the yarn between the two layers of fabric.
257 The stages of working a simple padded shape.
  (a) A second layer of net, used as the transparent fabric, held in place with the surface chain stitch outlining the shape to be padded.
  (b) Coloured yarn placed between the two layers of net.
  (c) Second layer of net cut away next to the surface chain stitches.
  (d) Second line of surface chain stitches worked alongside the first line.

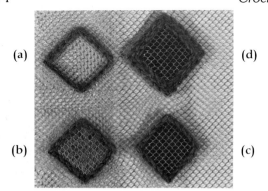

(a) (d)

(b) (c)

Felt shapes can be used in place of coloured yarn. The felt shape should be tacked onto the net prior to placing the second piece of transparent fabric into place. Cut surplus transparent fabric away from the outside of the shape when surface chain stitches have been worked round the shape.

Note The second piece of transparent fabric can be applied to either the right or the wrong side of the foundation fabric depending on the result required.

Surface crochet used as a neatening to a fabric edge

Net is used for the illustrated example of this technique. Other fabrics can be neatened in this way if a small crochet hook can be passed through the holes of the material requiring the neatening.

There are two methods shown:

(a) Cut the net first and work a surface stitch over the cut edge.

(b) Allow a hem allowance, cut the net and fold back on hem line. Work the surface stitches over the cut edge to secure.

258 Net fabric is cut away and an extended surface double crochet stitch worked along the cut edge. A chain stitch edging with picots is added to the double

crochet edging. A zigzag surface chain stitch line and a row of extended double crochet stitches complete the pattern.

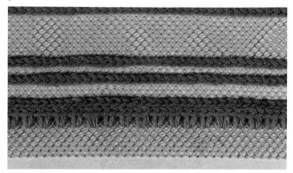

259 Net fabric turned back double to form a hemline. One row of extended double crochet stitches worked over the cut edge, with 4 additional rows of surface chain stitches placed at various intervals.

To conclude this chapter it seems worthwhile to mention that the technique of crochet on net is really a prior exercise to working onto fabrics, ie commercially woven, knitted or crochet fabrics. If this technique appeals to you, try working directly onto a woven material, using a frame and a fine hook and yarn. Once the technique is really mastered the designs may be worked very quickly. For large areas of fabric a slate embroidery frame is recommended. The slate frame leaves both hands free for working, as the frame is supported between two trestles or a substitute.

Finally, it must be stressed that surface crochet stitches can be very easily undone. It is therefore imperative that all work is secured firmly and neatly. All lines of stitches begin with a slip loop as explained for surface stitches on canvas. There are two ways to secure the yarn on completion of a line of stitches, and the one chosen will depend on the method of work being used. The last chain stitch can be secured by drawing the cut end through the last stitch, pulling the remaining yarn tightly and darning it into the work on the wrong side. Another method used when applying beads is a locked stitch. This is made by extending the loop on the hook 5 mm and inserting the hook again into the same position, placing yarn round hook and drawing the yarn up. Extend the loop as before and draw through loop already on hook. With the hook draw the first loop extended through the second extended loop and pull both loop on hook and working yarn tightly to lock the stitch. Cut yarn and darn into wrong side.

11 – Experimental crochet techniques

This chapter is really included as a diversion from generally accepted ideas about crochet. Included are some rather different ways in which the crochet hook can be used to achieve unusual and unexpected results. It is up to the reader to experiment with these ideas and apply the technique to whatever purpose she chooses. Some ideas would be useful to the embroideress, others are relevant to the making of garments and accessories. Some ideas use crochet fabric as the main feature, some incorporate another fabric which may be a commercially woven or knitted material, a hand-knitted fabric or a fabric made on a knitting machine. It is hoped that some of these ideas may inspire the use of crochet in a wider field than may be at first expected, linking the techniques with other materials and other methods of work when possible. The reason for this is the speed with which the surface crochet chain stitches can be worked and the satisfaction of creating something original. The surface crochet chain stitch forms the basis of the majority of ideas presented.

It is advisable for the reader to have read the two previous chapters on crochet on canvas and crochet on net before attempting the work in this chapter. Texture forms an important design feature in textiles, especially wall hangings. Many of the crochet techniques illustrated produce interesting textural shapes and raised work.

260 'Balls' and 'cups' feature in this example. The shapes are sewn onto a hessian backing and a chain stitch length worked in a very loopy yarn is sewn onto the backing between the shapes. To work the balls and cups (the cup is the reverse side of the ball):

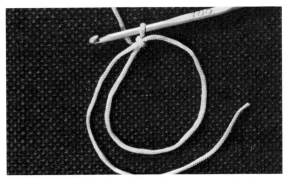

Centre round 261 Twist the yarn into a circle and work 1 chain stitch placing the hook into the circle and using the yarn from the spool or ball to work the chain stitch. Note the position of the cut end of yarn.

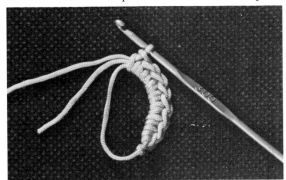

262 Continue placing hook into circle and work 8 double crochet.

263 Take the cut end of yarn and pull tightly until the circle is closed. Slip stitch into the first chain stitch to complete this round.
Round 2 1 chain to count as 1 double crochet. First double crochet is worked into 3rd stitch from hook. (2 double crochet into next stitch, 1 double crochet into next stitch) 4 times. Slip stitch into 1st chain stitch.
Round 3 1 chain to count as 1 double crochet. First double crochet is worked into 3rd stitch from hook. (2

double crochet into next stitch, 1 double crochet into next 2 stitches) 4 times. Slip stitch into first chain.

Round 4   1 chain to count as 1 double crochet. First double crochet is worked into 3rd stitch from hook. 1 double crochet into each stitch to end of round. Slip stitch into first chain. Continue in rounds until the required size is obtained. These shapes may be padded with cotton wool to form balls or inverted and left open for cups.

To make a larger size shape, work more stitches into the initial round; the following rounds, will of course, require more stitches.

264   Balls and cups are featured in this example with treble stitch coils and the Clones knot stitch. The background is hessian and the crochet pieces are sewn in place.

The coils are worked by placing several – 2, 3 or 4 – trebles into each stitch of a chain foundation length. These lengths can be varied and other stitches including double crochet, half treble and double treble can also be worked into the foundation chain to taper the length of the stitches. The coils have been applied in coiled circles to give a 'rosette' effect in this sample. The Clones knot is shown either side of the sample. The knot is worked between lengths of chain stitches.

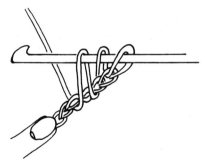

265   To work the knot stitch: work 12 chain approximately, *hold the chain length 1 cm below the

hook with the left hand and place yarn over hook. Place hook in front of chain length, yarn over hook and draw the yarn upwards in front of chain length*, repeat from * to * several times (10–18) depending on the size of the knot required. Insert hook into chain nearest hook, not covered with yarn, place yarn over hook and draw yarn through all loops on hook. Work 1 double crochet into chain stitch at base of knot to secure. See also Chapter 18. At least 6 chain stitches should be worked between each knot.

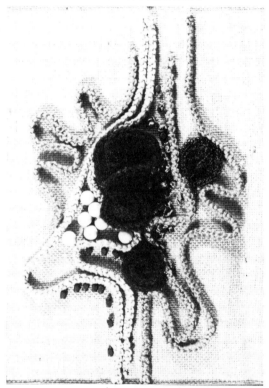

266   This example features the use of a crochet cord with coils. The cord forms an interesting line of textured crochet and follows the instructions on page 47. The cord is sewn to the background fabric.

267   This example features the use of coils; a varying degree of twist is shown and some coils have been opened out and some allowed to twist and hang freely. The degree of twist is made by altering the number of stitches worked into each foundation chain stitch.

268 Coils and petals are the only techniques illustrated. The petals are made: 20 chain, slip stitch into the 2nd stitch from hook placing hook into back single loop. Slip stitch into the next 18 stitches. Turn work, *miss 1 stitch, slip stitch into next 3 stitches placing hook into front single loop. 16 chain, slip stitch into 2nd stitch from hook, placing hook into back single loop, slip stitch into the next 18 stitches. Turn work*. Repeat from * to * for required number of petals.

269 A length of petals arranged in a cluster
270 A wall hanging using some of the crochet techniques explained. The hanging was designed and

worked by Karen Schueler. Couched and darned cotton and wools in serene blue tones contrast with a freeform shape of bright oranges, reds and yellows. Looped threads, appliquéd fabric and crocheted balls and scallops create high relief supported by bullion and French knots, padded satin stitch and rosette chain. The background is coarse Indian cotton with metallic thread, rayon cord, silk and raffia for accents.

Crochet fabric to hold padded shapes of leather

Crochet can be used to form a 'net' like a spider's web to be placed over other materials. Small open work crochet motifs worked in fine embroidery threads form a spider's web fabric which is placed over the padded leather shape.

271 A rectangular leather motif, slightly padded with felt below, with a crochet motif placed over the surface. The leather is pale blue, the crochet is silver. The sample forms part of an embroidered silver collar.

Simple embroidery stitches used on a double crochet background

Many simple embroidery stitches can be added to a base crochet fabric worked in double crochet. The crochet fabric is used as a counted thread material and the type and size of stitches used are controlled by the size of the double crochet stitch background, ie the yarn type and hook size.

272 Embroidery stitches:

(a)
(b)
(a)
(c)

(d)

(e)

(f)
(g)
(f)
(h)

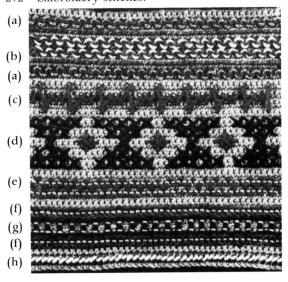

(a) Threaded herringbone – two colours used
(b) Two rows of threaded herringbone with a line of whipped running stitch on either side. The running stitch is the line of the double crochet
(c) Open Cretan stitch
(d) Cross stitch motifs with a 'star' cross stitch in the motif centres
(e) Threaded running stitch. The line of the double crochet forming the running stitch
(f) Pekinese stitch
(g) A variation of Guilloche stitch. Two colours used
(h) Stem stitch worked over a line of straight stitches – two colours used

For details on how to work the embroidery stitches see Barbara Snook, *Embroidery Stitches*, 1975.

Surface chain stitches as a decoration to a base fabric

The technique for working surface chain stitches was shown in Chapter 9. In this chapter the base fabric is either made in double crochet, or a crochet mesh or a loosely woven material, or a knitted fabric – either hand-knitted or machine-knitted.

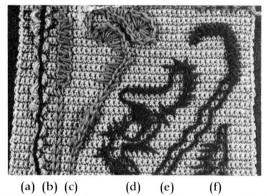

(a) (b) (c)   (d)   (e)   (f)

273   Surface chain stitches worked onto a base fabric of double crochet. Various modifications are made to the chain stitch:
(a) Surface chain stitch worked over 4 strands of another yarn. The strands are placed from side to side between the base fabric and the surface chain stitches to form a zigzag pattern. Each chain stitch secures the yarn in place
(b) A basic surface chain stitch leading into a broader chain stitch. This is worked by placing the hook and working 1 surface chain stitch first to the right (approximately 1 cm apart from the last stitch) and following this with 1 surface chain stitch immediately above. Repeat these 2 stitches to the left and so on. Variations in width can be made
(c) A basic surface chain stitch leading into a raised stitch. The crochet hook is placed into 4 different places, drawing the yarn through the fabric each time and extending the loop on the hook if necessary. The loop on the hook taken from the last hook insertion is drawn through all the other loops on the hook – thus completing the stitch. This is a very versatile stitch, and it will be found that many variations and shapes

can be made, depending on where the hook is inserted. An elongated surface double crochet stitch follows the raised stitch. Various curves are shown
(d) Further use of the elongated surface double crochet stitch with the zigzag surface chain worked horizontally
(e) Surface chain stitch worked diagonally, and the zigzag surface chain stitch worked back over the initial row to give a more raised line
(f) Spaced elongated surface double crochet stitches

Crochet stitches applied to a crochet mesh base fabric

Continuing the technique of working surface crochet stitches to a base fabric, even more textured and interesting designs can be worked onto a foundation fabric of a treble stitch mesh. This mesh can be made in a variety of ways, varying the size of the mesh according to the stitches used. The crochet mesh given in Chapter 3 for woven fabrics and the mesh used in filet crochet in Chapter 7 both make a suitable base fabric foundation. Surface stitches may incorporate double crochet, treble, double treble and so on. The stitches are worked from the right side of the crochet fabric. Designs to be worked may be charted onto graph paper and translated onto the crochet mesh. However, it must be remembered that the crochet mesh may not equate exactly with the graph paper and distortion of designs may occur. An alternative way of working a shape in this stitch is to use a paper or card template. The shape is then pinned onto the right side of the crochet foundation and the surface stitches worked round the edge. After the first row has been completed, the template can be removed and further surface stitches worked.

To work the surface treble stitch onto a mesh foundation: both yarn and hook are held above the fabric foundation and the surface stitches are worked from the right side. Place a slip loop on the hook and insert hook under a bar of the crochet mesh – either a chain stitch or a treble stitch. Place yarn over hook and draw the yarn through loop on hook – this secures the yarn onto the mesh. Work 3 chain to count as 1 treble. Work 2 more treble stitches placing hook right under the bars of the mesh for each stitch worked. Repeat the surface treble stitches working over the bars of the mesh in the direction of the design.

274   A band of surface treble stitches which could be

used as a decorative edging for a coat or jacket. It should be noted that the stitch uses a lot of yarn and adds weight to a garment. Some sagging or dropping may occur. To rectify any distortion in shape, a 'stay thread' should be placed along the vertical bars of the mesh foundation on the wrong side of the fabric. Each end of the stay thread should be secured after checking for correct length. Various colours and yarn types are featured in this illustration. The random shape uses different stitches which include surface double crochet, half treble and treble stitches. The number of stitches on each bar of the crochet mesh is increased to give a more ruched stitch.

Gathered, ruched and smocked fabrics

So far in this chapter the illustrations have featured crochet fabrics for the foundation of surface stitches. However, machine-knitted fabrics and hand-knitted fabrics can also be used for surface crochet. This technique could be incorporated into fashion garments forming a feature on sleeves and yoke lines. The idea used for these samples is to form a ruched and gathered fabric.

275 The fabric is made on a domestic knitting machine with a dropped stitch at regular intervals. This line of threads, formed by the dropped stitch leaves a line of horizontal threads. A contrasting yarn is held below the knitted fabric, the hook is held on the top – the right side. Surface chain stitches are worked over the line of vertical threads. To achieve a gathered effect, the surface chain stitches are worked over a number of vertical threads – eg 3–6, depending on the amount of gathering required. If the yarn used for this surface chain stitch has no elasticity, the fabric so formed will have the appearance of gathering, but no 'stretch' will be possible. But should the design need movement in the gathering, ie have some elasticity, the surface chain stitch should be worked in an elasticated yarn.

276 A smocked effect achieved by using a machine knitted base fabric and a silver elasticated yarn for surface chain stitches. The surface crochet is worked with both yarn and hook on the right side of the fabric. Make a slip loop and place on hook. Insert the hook along the line of the design, under 2 vertical lines of knitting, draw the yarn through the knitting and through the loop on the hook. Continue working through the knitting covering the line for the smocking. The chevron line is achieved by working 1 surface chain stitch with 3 loose chain stitches between, ie, chain stitches worked without the hook being inserted into the foundation fabric. The surface chain are worked in a zigzag line to form the chevron; the amount of knitting between each surface chain stitch can be gauged by counting the number of stitches between each surface chain stitch. The working yarn must be held on the right side in order to work this chevron.

Surface lines can be applied to a knitted foundation using an elasticated yarn held on the wrong side, with the hook on the right side and working lines of surface chain stitches. The tightness of the lines is gauged by the distance, ie the number of knitted stitches placed between each surface chain stitch. Lines may be straight, curved or zigzag.

Appliqué crochet work

Shapes worked in crochet can be applied and attached to a base fabric using surface crochet stitches.

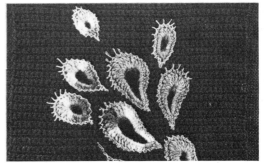

277 A tear drop motif attached with the elongated

surface double crochet stitch to a double crochet foundation fabric. The tear drop shape is made as follows: work a chain length, eg 12. Slip stitch into the first chain worked to form a circle. Insert the hook into the circle, work double crochet, half treble, treble, and half treble and double crochet stitches to form the tear drop shape. When the circle is covered, mould the stitches to the desired shape by pinning onto the crochet base. Work the elongated surface double crochet stitch all round the edge of the shape inserting the hook into the foundation fabric and then into the tear drop shape. For further motifs which could be used for appliqué see Chapter 13.

Quilting using crochet stitches

Two pieces of fabric, such as crochet, hand/machine knitted fabric or a loosely woven material are required for quilting. The quilting technique gives a firm, thick fabric with lines of stitching forming indentations on the surface. Usually a wadding is used between the two pieces of material to achieve this effect. The quilted lines are worked with surface chain stitches placed through both pieces of fabric, along a given design line. The wadding is placed between the fabrics, but there can be some difficulty in passing the hook through the wadding. If difficulty occurs, work the surface chain stitch through the two layers of fabric along the first line of the design, place a strip of wadding between the fabrics close to the chain stitching. Work another row of surface chain stitches. This second line will enclose the wadding in a 'tube'. Repeat along the fabric until all the lines of the design have been worked. These instructions apply to quilt-

ing a design in straight or curved lines forming channels, a suitable design for this type of work. However, enclosed shapes can be worked too, by working the surface chain stitches along three-quarters of the shape, placing wadding into the shape and completing the outline. The design for quilting may be tacked onto the right side of the fabric, using a template of the shape as a guide line. Careful pinning and tacking should control the fabric while working the surface chain stitches. However, only the pinning method can be used if the wadding is put into place after each line of the design is worked.

278 A small quilted bag, featuring a fan-shape design and double crochet stitches to finish the scalloped edge. Double crochet is also used to join the gusset shape which is not quilted. The foundation fabric is knitted. The quilting is highlighted by using a silver yarn

12 – Aran-style crochet

Most people associate Aran work with knitted garments. Using crochet techniques, some of which have been featured in previous chapters, Aran textured fabrics can be quickly made. Once the basic Aran stitches have been learnt, many variations and designs can be worked, using coloured yarns in a variety of ways. Normally Aran garments are worked in a natural off-white yarn (see colour plate 1, facing page 92).

Crochet stitches used to produce an Aran-style fabric

Surface chain stitch and surface double crochet stitches form the main features of Aran designs worked in crochet. The surface stitches give a raised relief texture to the crochet fabric.

Surface chain and double crochet stitches have been explained in previous chapters. It will be noticed that surface double crochet stitch stands in greater relief than the chain stitch.

279 and 280   The working of surface double crochet

onto a crochet fabric worked throughout in double crochet stitch. Place a slip loop on the hook. Hold the yarn below work (the wrong side) and insert hook from the right side along the line of the pattern. Place yarn over hook and draw yarn through fabric and through loop on hook. *Insert hook into same position as last hook insertion, yarn over hook and draw yarn through fabric (279). Insert hook in next space above last stitch, working along the line of the pattern, place yarn over hook and draw yarn through fabric (280) and through both loops on hook*, repeat from * to * until the pattern is complete. Secure end of yarn at end of line.

It should be noted that each surface chain stitch is worked over 1 double crochet stitch. Designs for Aran patterns can be charted onto graph paper, drawing in the lines and positions for the surface stitches and the textured areas. The surface stitches are placed over the double crochet foundation, the vertical lines of the graph paper represent the vertical line of the double crochet stitch, ie the base of the stitch. The horizontal lines of the graph paper represent the horizontal line, or top of the stitch (48).

The surface stitches can be twisted in waves, crossed to form a cable effect, or just straight.

281   A wave in 2 lines; also a double twisted wave, 1 line being worked over another. It will be seen that 1 line lies above the other throughout the sample, 1 separate yarn being required for each line. The twisted or cabled effect can be achieved by working the 2 lines simultaneously, and placing the yarn from the right-hand side over the yarn on the left-hand side when the 2 lines meet.

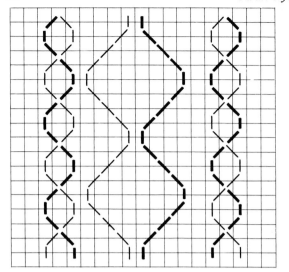

282 Graph design for working surface stitching in crochet

Berry stitch

The berry texture forms a very characteristic feature of Aran work.

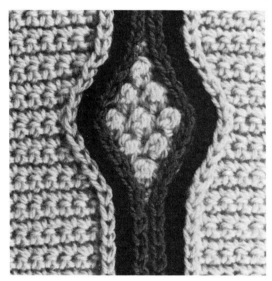

283 A group of 9 berry stitches between 3 lines of surface double crochet on both sides. Berry stitch is worked between rows of double crochet at the required position for the pattern. To work the berry stitch: 3 double crochet stitches are required to work the berry stitch over. Slip stitch into the first stitch, yarn over hook and insert hook into next stitch, yarn over hook and draw through yarn, yarn over hook and draw yarn through *first loop only* on hook. Yarn over hook and insert hook into same stitch, yarn over hook and draw through yarn, yarn over hook and draw through all 5 loops on hook. 1 chain stitch. Slip stitch into next stitch. 1 berry stitch has been made.

On the return row, work 1 double crochet into the slip stitch, 1 slip stitch into the double crochet and 1 double crochet into the slip stitch. *Note* The chain stitch is missed. To form a really textured berry stitch, keep the yarn fairly loose for the main loop stitch, but very tight for the slip stitches.

Berry stitch may be worked as an all over textured fabric, or in groups. Often the groups are placed between lines of surface chain, or surface double crochet stitches as the example illustrated.

284 Moss stitch

Moss stitch produces another very textured crochet fabric which is used to imitate the Aran textures. Moss stitch can be worked to form an even or uneven pattern. The uneven moss stitch forms a pleasing all over textured effect and this stitch is featured in the panels of the cream coat (colour plate 1, facing page 92).

To work moss stitch: 2 stitches are required to work this stitch over.
Row 1 Slip stitch into the first stitch, 1 half treble into next stitch.
Row 2 Work 1 half treble into the slip stitch and slip stitch into the half treble.

Even moss stitch is made by repeating these 2 rows so that the raised and textured stitches form vertical lines. The uneven moss stitch produces a more interesting effect and this is formed by working a third and fourth row, reversing the instructions for the first and second rows.

285 Ribbed double crochet

This stitch was shown in detail in Chapter 2. A very useful crochet technique which produces an excellent textured fabric. The edge panel is worked in this stitch on the panel coat shown in colour plate 1, facing page 92.

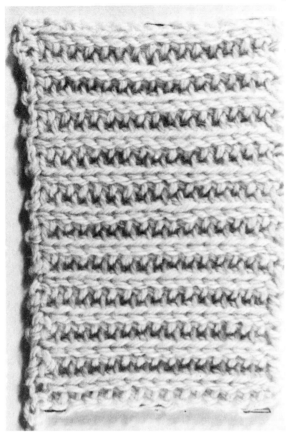

285

13 – Circular crochet

The making of circles for motifs and circular patterns and designs has been referred to in previous chapters. The technique forms an important method of work which will be required in the making of many projects. The details for making circles and some of the problems involved are explained in this chapter. The technique can be applied to the making of either individual motifs which are joined together (this was mentioned in Chapter 6) or for the construction of circular articles such as hats, shawls, skull caps, bags, boots/shoes and socks etc.

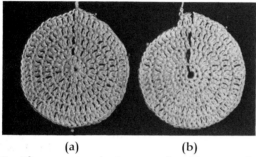

(a)   (b)

286   There are two basic ways of making a circle:
  (a)   constructing complete circles
  (b)   working in a continuous spiral
For both methods the crochet is usually worked one way, ie no turning at the end of a round.

The main problem of working in circles is judging the amount of increased stitches to work on each new round in order for the work to lie flat, ie not fluted and not cupped.

It is possible to calculate the exact number of stitches required on a circle if the diameter of the circle is known. The formula is:
Circumference = 2 πr. ($\pi = \frac{22}{7}$ or 3.143)
The radius (r) is half the known diameter (eg let r = 14 cm). If the stitch count is 3 trebles measure 2 cm, the calculation would be:
$2 \times \frac{22}{7} \times 14 = 88$ cm. Therefore the number of trebles required for a circle with a diameter of 28 cm would be:
$\frac{88}{2} \times 3 = 132$ trebles.

(a)   Constructing circles in complete rounds

The sample shows the circle worked in treble stitch, but any other stitch may be used applying the same principles.
Round 1   4 chain. Join to the first chain worked with a slip stitch to form a circle.
Round 2   Work 3 chain to count as 1 treble. Work 11 treble, placing the hook into the centre of the chain stitch circle. Slip stitch into the 3rd chain to complete circle.
  If you have difficulty in deciding which is the right

chain stitch, place a safety pin (mark A) into the 3rd chain stitch before starting to work the following trebles of the round. On completion of the round, it will be quite clear into which stitch the slip stitch should be placed.
Round 2   3 chain to count as 1 treble. Place a safety pin into the 3rd chain stitch just worked (mark B). Work 2 treble into the next stitch after mark A. Work 2 treble into each treble of previous round. 1 treble into stitch before mark A (ie there will be 12 pairs of treble stitches including the 3 chain at start of round). Slip stitch into 3rd chain – mark B.
Round 3   3 chain to count as 1 treble. 1 treble into next stitch after mark B. 2 treble into next stitch. *1 treble into next stitch, 2 treble into next stitch*, repeat from * to * 10 times. 1 treble into next stitch. 1 treble into stitch before mark B. Slip stitch into 3rd chain at start of round. There should be 36 trebles in total, including the 3 chain at start of round.

To continue to work a flat circle, repeat Round 3 by working 1 more single treble stitch between each increased stitch for every new round.

Some difficulties which may occur when working in circles:
1   The fabric may flute, ie too many stitches have been worked on each round. Check the number of increased stitches.
2   The fabric may curl upwards forming a cupped or tubed construction, ie too few stitches have been worked on each round. Check the number of increased stitches.
3   The size of the centre circle made by the chain stitches at the beginning can cause either of these problems if the following rounds are not geared to the size of this initial circle. If the number of chains formed at the beginning is increased, a larger circle will be made and more trebles will have to be placed into this initial circle. The following circles will require a proportionate increase of stitches.
4   The size of the hook can also influence these problems, ie the tension of the stitches being either too loose or too tight. If this is the cause of the problem, re-check the calculations.
5   The height of each stitch pattern can also be the cause of problems. Some people work treble stitch to form a deeper or higher stitch, thus making the final circumference of the circle larger. Again check your calculations.

Light pressing after blocking into shape often improves circular work – see Chapter 17.

(b) Circles formed by working in continuous spirals

The centre and start of the circle should be made as for

(a), that is by working 4 chain, slip stitch into the first chain to form a circle, then work 8 double crochet into the circle. No steps are made and no rising chains at the start of each round; simply continue working into each stitch continuously. Work 2 double crochet into the next 8 stitches. In order to know how many spirals have been worked, it is wise to mark with a safety pin the last stitch worked on each complete spiral. The dark thread marks the end of each spiral in the photograph. If a larger stitch is required, eg a treble, it will be better to work gradually into this deeper stitch by working from the double crochet, to half treble, then the treble as follows. This will avoid a stepped result. Continue to work into each stitch by working: (1 double crochet into next stitch, 2 double crochet into next stitch) 4 times, (1 half treble in next stitch, 2 half treble into next stitch) twice. (1 treble in next stitch, 2 treble into next stitch) 14 times. 4 spirals now covered. Continue working in spirals increasing by 1 the number of single trebles worked between each increase on each new spiral.

Working in spirals will leave a step when the shape is complete. To avoid a step, work 2 or 3 half trebles, followed by 2 or 3 double crochet before ending work with 2 slip stitches. There will still be a small irregular line on the outer shape of the circle.

If a fluted effect is wanted while working in the spiral method, begin the circle with 16 stitches into the centre hole and work more increased stitches depending on the amount of fluting required.

For a tube effect, work 2 or 3 rounds in the spiral technique explained followed by several spirals with no increased stitches.

For suggestions for using the circular techniques with ideas for designing and methods of working the articles shown see Chapter 17, Working methods.

To make a circular shape square

Sometimes it is necessary to use a circle to form the centre of a square shape for patchwork motifs. The method of making a circle square is to divide the circle into 4 sections from the centre; therefore a start of 12 trebles makes the division simple. When the round is reached in which the square shape is to be formed, on each of the 4 sections an extra increase in the stitch length and number of stitches will be needed. For example, into 1 stitch forming the corner work: (1 treble, 1 double treble, 3 chain, 1 double treble, 1 treble), at 4 regular intervals round the circle.

Other methods of starting a circular shape

287   Rings of various sizes placed onto a ruched satin

for a textured quality. The rings are sewn in place. Compare with the rings used in Chapter 6, (figure 210).

288   Several rings covered with double crochet and held together with petersham ribbon laced between the rings. Brass rings form the base.

289   A variety of motifs based on the circular theme, including oval and square shapes.

290   Leather circles with crochet placed into holes made into the leather. Double crochet, half treble, treble stitches and double treble stitches have been worked to give a graduated line to form a crescent shape to the crochet edges. All the shapes illustrated in the last two photographs can be used as the centre of circular work, or each piece can form part of a patchwork fabric. Further motifs are also illustrated in Chapter 18, Irish crochet.

Ideas for circular work

291 (*overleaf*)   A summer hat made in Twilley's *Stalite* yarn, based on the circular technique. The spaces and treble stitch are the main pattern features in this hat. Millinery wire is placed in the outer edge of the brim to hold the shape.

292 (*below*)   A cotton d'oiley made in the 1920s. A very fine piece, made with even and consistent stitches. This could be a starting point for designing a more open work style shawl using a coarser yarn and a

larger hook size. Ideas for working cushion covers and circular bed covers and wall hangings could derive from an old example of crochet work.

293   A white cotton skull cap of the type worn by Muslim Arabs under their white headdress (*kaffiya*). These caps may be bought in the Far East, and some are imported into the States of the Arabian Gulf having been made in India and Pakistan. They are also to be seen in Turkey worn without any further headdress. Again, this cap could be used as a starting point for a circular design. It features a decorative shell edge.

Flower loom crochet

Crochet is not usually associated with flower loom work. However, by working the surface chain stitch technique, a quick and efficient flower loom motif can be made. The motifs can be used in place of the circular crochet motifs mentioned previously and for the patchwork shapes used for making fabrics (Chapter 6). They can also be used in place of the hairpin motifs which are described in the following chapter.

There are two types of looms available: the square and the circular shape. Both types have a series of two rows of 12 pegs. The square produces an easier shape to join together if a closed fabric is to be aimed for, and the circular shape can be modified with additional crochet to form a square if wanted. Circles can be joined using crochet stitches – Chapter 17, Working methods. The loom when purchased will have clear directions for placing the yarn over the pegs. Both rows of pegs may be covered, or just the outer row as in the examples.

294   The yarn is placed to and fro covering each outer peg approximately 3–6 times depending on the thread used. A mesh will be formed over the centre hole of the loom. The yarn is then secured by using a bodkin and a sewing stitch. However, surface chain stitches are quicker to work and will form an effective finish. The illustration shows the working of the first round of chain stitches on the circular loom. The square loom shows 2 rounds of chain stitches with an extended stitch placed in the centre of the shape. To work the surface crochet: thread the loom as directed.

294

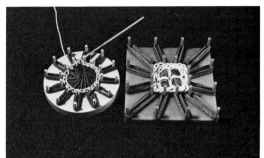

Work the crochet from the peg side of the loom with a matching or contrasting yarn. Make a slip loop and remove from hook. Insert hook into the space alongside a loom peg. Place slip loop onto hook. *Insert hook into next space between pegs, yarn over hook and draw yarn through loom and through loop on hook*, repeat from * to * to complete circle. Several rounds of surface chain stitches can be worked continuously. When the crochet is complete, cut the yarn and secure before removing the shape from the loom. Flower loom motifs can be sewn together to form a fabric. Alternately, a chain stitch length can be worked round the outer loops of the flower, with a double crochet stitch into each group of loops as they come off the loom pegs.

295 To form a sharp corner shaping, 4 double crochet stitches should be placed into each corner loop. These squares may be sewn together, or joined together with double crochet stitches – see Chapter 17, Working methods. In the illustration, two motifs have additional chain stitches around the outer edge, two are left un-worked. The joining of motifs can be worked at the same time as the chain stitches are worked onto the loops around the edge of the flower. To work this type of join, complete the edge of one flower, and start to work around a second flower.

295

When you reach the position to join, insert hook over chain stitches of the first flower and work 1 chain stitch, then continue working around the second flower and repeat joining chain stitch when required.

Flower loom shapes may be used individually as applied decoration onto a base fabric or 'en masse' after joining to form an ideal fabric for shawls, stoles, scarves and bedcovers.

14 – Hairpin crochet

Hairpin crochet is a further technique allied to crochet work. The equipment required for hairpin crochet includes the crochet hook, yarn and a U-shaped prong known as a hairpin crochet prong. These prongs are shaped like a hairpin, and the distance between the two prongs can vary between 10 mm and 100 mm.[4] This governs the width of braid which is ultimately made using the prong. Another type of hairpin is available which can be adjustable – this consists of two lengths of steel rods and two blocks of wood or plastic containing holes at regular intervals. These blocks hold and control the rods. A home-made substitute of this type is shown in Chapter 5, Cords and fringes.

The method of working on the hairpin prongs is simple: the yarn is wound round the prongs, and a primary crochet stitch is worked to hold the yarn in place. The prongs are rotated, the yarn is wound round and more stitches worked. Hairpin crochet produces strips of fabric with loops on each side. These strips can be used for decoration on fashion garments or articles of soft furnishing. Because of the loops produced, hairpin work is ideal for fringes.

The strips can be formed into circles by threading a yarn through the loops on one side and drawing up tightly. The circles can then be treated as a motif and joined together to form a fabric. A mohair shawl made in two sizes of circles is shown in colour plate 3 (between pages 92/3). The working details appear in Chapter 17. The strips can also be joined together, in strips, using a variety of crochet stitches to form a fabric.

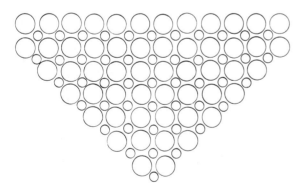

296 Diagram to show the positioning of the hairpin circles for the mohair shawl.

It is the choice and position of the crochet stitches used to form the strips, the crochet selected to join the work, and the type of yarn chosen which can turn a very basic crochet technique into something which can be much more interesting than might at first be expected.

297 A white cotton d'oiley edged with hairpin work made during the 1920s. The hairpin strip is curved by the use of additional crochet chain stitches and double crochet. The outer edge is scalloped and the crochet is worked directly onto the hairpin loops. The inner edge also worked onto the hairpin loops is drawn in by decreasing to fit onto the fabric centre. The lace edging is sewn onto the fabric.

The basic hairpin techniques

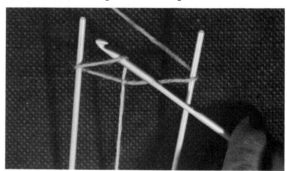

298 Hold the hairpin in the left hand and the yarn in the normal way. Make a slip loop and place on left-hand prong – leave the loop open. Wind the yarn in front of the right-hand prong and take behind the hairpin. Insert hook under the slip loop.

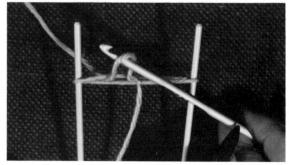

299 Place yarn over hook and draw through yarn.

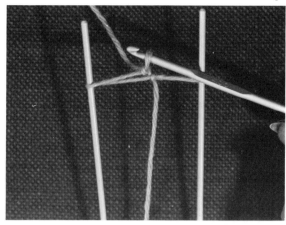

300   Work 1 chain stitch – do not remove hook. *Turn hairpin round, right side to left side as you would turn the page of a book. To do this you have to lift the crochet hook over the top of the prong, and the yarn will be placed in front of the prong which is now placed on the right-hand side.

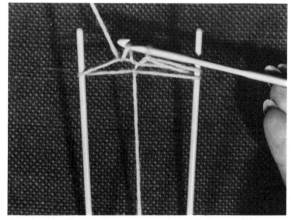

301   Place hook under front loop of yarn on left-hand prong, yarn over hook.

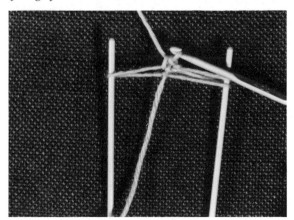

302   Yarn over hook and draw through both loops on hook, ie 1 double crochet stitch has been worked*, repeat from * to * for required length.

(a)   (b)

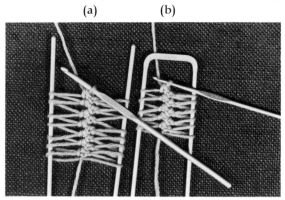

303   Two different methods of holding the hairpin prong:
(a)   The open end upwards. By holding the hairpin in this manner, it is easier to turn the hairpin and work the double crochet stitches in the centre. The disadvantage is the need to remove all the loops when the prongs are covered and replacing the top loop when working a long strip.
(b)   The closed end upwards. If the open end is placed downwards, when the prongs are covered, the excess loops just fall away and a long strip can be easily worked. The disadvantage, however, is the need to remove the crochet hook each time the hairpin is turned. Slip the hook from the stitch, turn the hairpin and re-insert the hook, from the front, into the stitch. If the hook is not removed before turning, you will find your hook on the back of the hairpin and it will be almost impossible to work the double crochet stitch.

Joining the strips

304   Three strips joined together using a basic technique. Place 2 strips side by side, insert the hook into 1 loop on one side, and draw through 1 loop from the other strip. Continue drawing loops through each other, working from side to side. One or 2 loops can be worked each time.

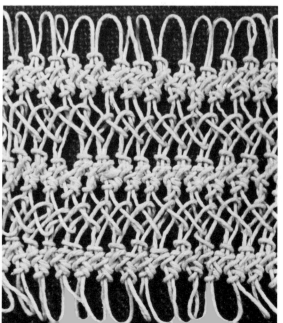

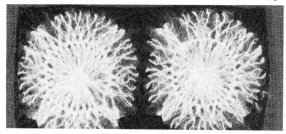

305   Two circles formed by drawing together the loops on one side. These are secured firmly in the centre. Chain stitches, half trebles and trebles have been used to 'square off' the circle prior to joining.

   Try the simple techniques shown placing the stitch to one side of the prong – this will produce a real fringed effect. Experiment by working with different stitches over the loops, and try one yarn using the same stitches but on different sized hairpin prongs. The very narrow prong if used with a very thick yarn will form an excellent type of braid with few or no loops on each side.

Variations on the basic techniques

306 (a)   Basic technique, using two hairpins and a tubular rayon cord. One narrow prong (40 mm) and one wider prong (80 mm) are held together with one prong from each hairpin lying together. The double crochet stitches are worked between the prongs of the narrow hairpin, and the cord is placed round the wider prong every third complete hairpin rotation.

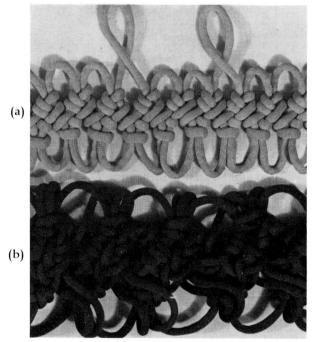

(a)

(b)

306 (b)   Variation on the double crochet stitches using a tubular rayon cord. Place the slip loop on the left-hand prong (place yarn round right-hand prong, front to back, 1 double crochet under front single loop

of left prong) 3 times. *Turn prong, yarn will be placed in front of prong and behind the prong now on the right. Work 1 double crochet under front 3 loops of left-hand prong (yarn round right prong, front to back, 1 double crochet under front 3 loops of left-hand prong) twice*, repeat from * to * for required length. This method of working 3 loops on the right-hand prong and 3 double crochet before turning the hairpin makes a much more dense braid. Try using a narrower hairpin and a chenille type yarn – the braid formed will have smaller and closer loops on each side.

307   Two variations using rayon tubular yarn and raffia.

(a)   Place a slip loop on the left-hand prong, yarn round right prong, front to back, work 1 double crochet under front loop of left prong placing the stitch as near to left prong as possible. Turn prong. *Insert hook under single front loop of left prong, yarn over hook and draw through yarn, yarn over hook and insert hook under single front loop of left prong, yarn over hook and draw through yarn, yarn over hook and draw through all 4 loops on hook. Turn prong. 1 double crochet under front single loop of left hand prong, placing stitch as near to left prong as possible. Turn prong,* repeat from * to * for required length. To form a firm straight edge: slip stitch along the side with the short loops. If a wider hairpin is used a longer fringe will be formed.

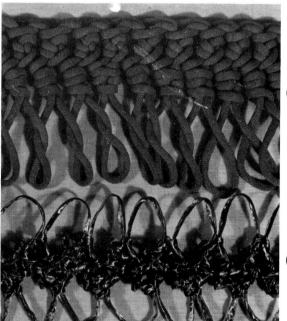

(a)

(b)

(b)   Worked as (a) placing the double crochet in the centre. Work 1 double crochet, 1 treble, 1 double crochet into the front single loop for each turn of the hairpin.

308   A basic braid with extended fringing. An additional cut length of yarn is looped through the loops of one side of the braid to form a fringing. The yarn is used double for the additional loops.

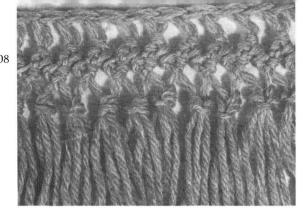

309 Diagram to show the method for adding the fringe. A slip stitch straightens the opposite side.

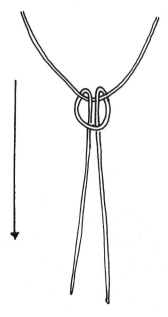

Hairpin crochet using beads

Beads may be incorporated into the braid by placing the beads onto the yarn prior to working the crochet. See Chapter 9 for the method of transferring beads.

310 Two simple examples of hairpin braid using beads.

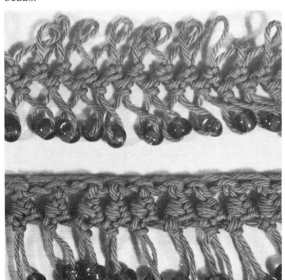

The hairpin prong can be used to produce unusual textures such as a pointed petal effect.

311 and 312 Hairpin crochet worked to form petal shaping. The stitch used is double crochet, and the hairpin is *not rotated*. The sample shown is worked with a DK yarn, a 50 mm prong and a No. 4.00 ISR

crochet hook. Place slip loop on left-hand prong and make 1 chain. The yarn should be behind the prong. *Extend the stitch on hook and place onto right-hand prong. Wrap the yarn in front of left-hand prong and over right-hand prong 4 times. Place hook downwards between the 5 loops on right-hand prong.

313 Catch the yarn and draw upwards.

314   Place hook in front of loops and catch the yarn

on hook. Yarn over hook and draw through both loops on hook. Work 9 double crochet over top 5 loops. Place hook *between* the top 4 loops on left-hand prong, yarn over hook and draw yarn up. Yarn over hook and draw through both loops on hook,* repeat from * to * for required length.

Hairpin crochet using groups of beads to form a berry edging

Beads should be placed onto the yarn before starting the crochet.
315 and 316   This edging features groups of beads with double crochet.
315   The braid when the hairpin prongs are removed

316   One double crochet stitch is worked into each group of threads opposite the beads, and 5 chain stitches are worked between each group.

The beads are wood and measure about 6 mm in diameter; a fine string 1 mm thick, a 40 mm hairpin prong and a No. 2.00 ISR crochet hook were used for this sample. The hairpin is always turned right side towards the left side.
Work 4 chain. Place first chain worked onto right-hand prong and leave yarn behind the hairpin.
317   *Place 7 beads against the left-hand prong 3 towards the back and 4 to the front and turn hairpin.

318   1 chain. (Place yarn behind left-hand prong and turn hairpin. 1 double crochet in back loop of left-hand prong – that is the loop with the beads. Yarn round left-hand prong placing 7 beads over prong and turn hairpin. 1 double crochet in back loop of left-hand prong) twice. 3 double crochet over top loops above chain stitches on left side. 1 double crochet *between* loops on left prong. Yarn round left prong and turn hairpin. 3 chain.* Repeat from * to * for required length

1   The textured crochet used for
this Tibetan panel coat was inspired
by Aran-style crochet stitches.
Thirty 50 gm balls of Patons and
Baldwins *Capstan* yarn for Aran
knitting in shade No. 50 would be
required and a No. 4.50 ISR crochet
hook, which produces a firm fabric.
The design for the coat is based on
Folkwear Ethnic Paper Patterns
No. 118, which is a design taken from
a twelfth-century sleeveless coat. It
makes an ideal shape for crochet
and the various panels are worked
in different textured stitches. The
panels are joined together by sewing
and a surface chain stitch is used to
highlight the line of the two centre
panels. The method of working to a
paper pattern shape is explained in
detail in Chapter 17, page 106

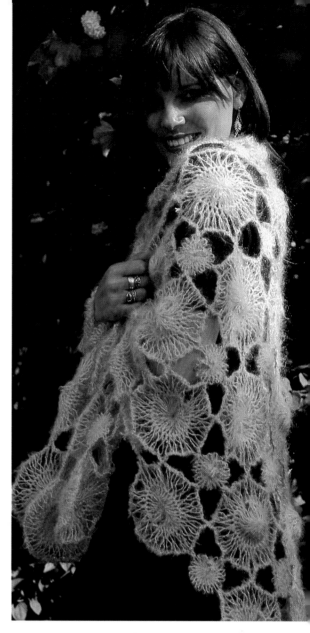

2   A jerkin made in Patons and Baldwins *Fiona* yarn using 20 squares to form the main area: four rows of three squares for the back, and one row of four squares for each front. Two strips of white ribbing worked in trebles in relief—one 14 cm wide for the neck edge, and one 7 cm wide for the waistline trim—complete the jerkin. Six ball buttons fasten the fronts and fit through the treble stitches. The jerkin would require: two 50 gm balls Ailsa Blue (colour A in the instructions on pages 55-56); two 50 gm balls Sky Mixture—6404 (colour B); two 50 gm balls white—504 (colour C). Three 50 gm balls of white would be required in addition for the ribbing. Each square should measure 15 cm. Recommended hook size No. 4.00 ISR

3   The basic hairpin crochet technique is used for this shawl. Twelve 25 gm balls of Jaeger mohair *Spin Glitter Moonbeam* yarn in shade 42 were chosen for this design. The shawl measures approximately 185 cm x 100 cm. Forty-seven circles measuring 5 cm in diameter and 54 measuring 13 cm form the shape. Two sizes of prongs — 20.00 mm and 80.00 mm — are recommended for the circles. For detailed working instructions, see page 93

Right
4   Freely worked crochet bolero using gold leather and a variety of stitches. The method of working is explained on page 117 and the outline is shown in figure 371

5   A variety of Irish crochet motifs
using Coats mercer crochet yarn
sewn onto a background fabric,
showing a modern application of
Irish crochet techniques. For
working instructions, see page 136

Right
6   An oya 150 years old worn by
Niyaz Büyükaksoy, the niece of
Nezihe Araz. The design is known
as the flower of the seven mountains
(the Aydin Region)

Left

7 A simplified Irish crochet technique using a variety of Twilley's yarns to produce individual circles in different sizes. The circles are sewn together to form a basic bolero shape. See page 137

8 A very special kese, made in black silk and gold thread, belonging to Nadide Uluant. On the side illustrated is the *tura* or 'signature' of the Sultan, which gives his name, together with that of his father, and ends with the words 'he is always victorious': 'Abdul Aziz Han bin Mahmut Han el Muzaffer Daima'. On the reverse (not illustrated) is the name of the pupil who made the kese, with the date: 'Amelu'l — Fakir Elfi Kostantimyye —1289'. The dating is in Rumi years, in which 1289 is the equivalent of about 1868. The kese was made in Istanbul

9 Green oya called 'eyelashes'. Property of Nezihe Araz

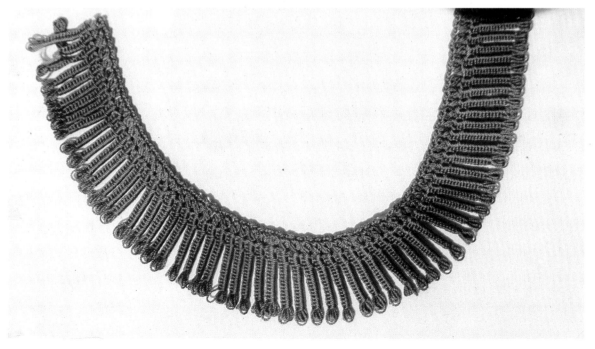

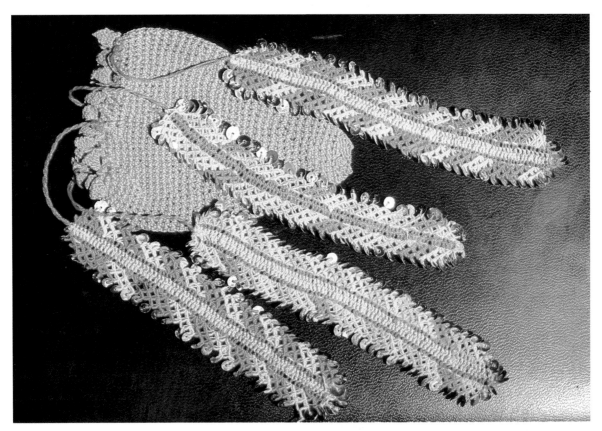

10 Turquoise blue crochet purse with decorated cord ends made with needlemade techniques and crochet stitches. Property of Nadide Uluant

11 A ring with a crochet surround made using the technique described on page 98. It has been placed onto a commercially made ring base. The stone is a piece of quartz polished in a domestic stone polishing machine

of braid, remove hairpin each time the prongs are full.
319   A simple braid using two different yarns. The hairpin is *not rotated*. Yarn A is mohair, yarn B is a shiny yarn.

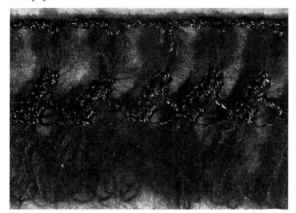

With yarn A make a slip loop and extend to fit over both prongs. Remove hook and leave yarn behind prong. Place yarn in front of right-hand prong from back to front, over left-hand prong from front to back, 3 times. Leave the yarn behind the hairpin. With yarn B work 6 double crochet over all loops just formed by yarn A and leave hook in the last stitch made. *Place yarn A round both prongs 3 times, continuing in the same direction as before. Extend the stitch on hook and place on right-hand prong. Remove hook and place between loops made by yarns A and B on right-hand side of work, yarn B over hook and draw through yarn. Work 3 double crochet over top 3 loops made

with yarn A and 1 loop in yarn B. Work 3 double crochet over top 3 loops made with yarn A and 1 single thread of yarn B*. Repeat from * to * for required length removing hairpin prongs as necessary. A length of chain stitches can be worked to secure the yarn B in the same way as the last sample. The group of 6 double crochet can be centred between the two prongs.

This basic technique of using two yarns without rotating the hairpin has many possibilities and is worth exploring.

The last three examples of hairpin crochet illustrated in this chapter have originated from examples of Turkish hairpin work, see Chapter 19. Colour plate 3, between pages 92/3, shows a shawl made using the basic hairpin crochet technique. It requires 12 × 25 gm balls of Jaeger mohair *Spin Glitter Moonbeam* yarn in shade 42. The shawl measures approximately 185 cm × 100 cm. The shape is formed by 47 circles measuring 5 cm and 54 circles measuring 13 cm in diameter. Two sizes of prongs – 20 mm and 80 mm are recommended for the circles.

The length of the braid made for the 5 cm circles requires 24 loops on each prong, and the 13 cm circles require 32 loops on each prong. On completion of each length, it is important to secure and anchor together the first stitch made and the last stitch made before cutting yarn and forming into the circle. Thread a separate length of yarn through all loops on one side of the braid and secure with knot (see figure 374, page 119). The circles are laid out as shown in figure 296, page 88 and the crochet method of joining the motifs is explained in Chapter 17, page 120.

15 – Crochet using unusual materials

Most people associate crochet with yarns alone, and so far in this book yarns of various types have been the main material used. Beads have been illustrated in some of the techniques as additional extras but in this section, beads, stones, shells, metallic yarn and wire are the main feature of the work.

Beads with crochet, used as the main feature

There are three methods of working with beads using crochet:

(a) Place the beads on the yarn used for the crochet prior to starting work.
(b) Place the beads on a secondary yarn or yarns.
(c) Sew the beads onto the crochet fabric when completed.

(a) Beads placed onto the working yarn

Transfer the beads onto the working yarn, see Chapter 9. The technique requires careful planning as the beads must be the correct size for the yarn being used and measure roughly the same size as 1 double crochet stitch. The method is most suitable for one-colour beaded designs, but two or more colours may be used. This does require more skill and a charted graph design prepared beforehand. All the different colours should be indicated. For each line of crochet, the order of beads in their correct colour sequence would need to be noted and the beads threaded onto the crochet yarn in this order. Therefore only simple repeat patterns are possible. If the colour sequence is very complicated, with three or more bead colours required, separate yarns should be used for each colour and a jacquard method followed. When threading a beaded pattern in colour sequence, remember that they would be used in reverse order.

320   A small beaded sovereign purse dated c 1850

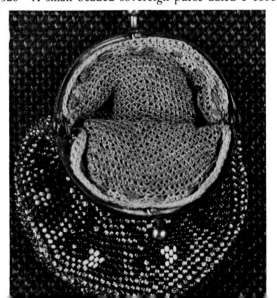

worked in this technique. Double crochet stitch is used throughout, and these stitches are clearly visible in the illustration although no crochet is seen on the beaded side.

Method of working with beads on yarn to follow a set pattern   Work out your pattern very accurately on graph paper and place the beads onto the yarn. Let 1 square on the graph paper represent 1 bead and 1 double crochet stitch. For each square requiring a bead, work 1 double crochet stitch: insert hook into next stitch, yarn over hook and draw through yarn. Place 1 bead close to work, yarn over hook and draw through both loops on hook. For squares without beads, if required, simply work 1 double crochet with no bead.

If more than 1 bead is placed for each double crochet worked, a looped effect will result.

(a)  (b)

321   Two reticules of c 1850 using silk yarn and beads. The beads have been placed to form a repeat pattern and much of the silk is visible between the beaded areas. The reticule on the left (a) has three colours of beads, and the pattern is worked by following the chart in double crochet working the yarns in the correct order to give the right colour bead as indicated on the charted design. Yarns not in use should be carried inside the double crochet stitches – see figure 229, page 64, which shows double crochet being worked over another cord. Using this technique, loops will be avoided on the wrong side. When designing an article using this technique it is wise to have beads of two colours only on one row.

The reticule on the right (b), is made in double crochet with cut steel beads in one colour.

Points to note when working beads using this technique:

1   Beads must contain a hole the right size in order to be placed onto the crochet yarn.

2   Beads must be of the right diameter in order to cover the area of 1 double crochet stitch.

3   It is best to plan a design to be worked in double crochet worked one way, ie break the yarn at the end

of each row, and rejoin yarn at the start of last row without turning work. It is advisable to plan designs requiring circular shapes, and the double crochet can then be worked in continuous spirals.

4 Double crochet stitches are usually worked by placing hook into the back single loop of each stitch. This places the beads in a better position on the fabric surface.

(b) Beads placed onto a secondary yarn or yarns

A thin strong yarn can be used, as it will not show in the fabric, selecting a different coloured yarn for each colour of bead used. Transfer the beads onto the yarn. Ideally, the yarn should match the colour of the bead. Plan the pattern for the bead work on graph paper. Work in double crochet stitch letting each square on the graph paper represent 1 double crochet stitch, with or without a bead as indicated. 'One-way' double crochet produces a better beaded surface than crochet worked to and fro.

The method of working with beads on a secondary yarn is to work the double crochet stitches over the yarns containing the beads, as for working over cords, explained in Chapter 8. When a bead is required, place 1 bead into place and continue working over the cords.

322 and 323 A sample using this method and the charted pattern for it. Each symbol represents a different colour. The pattern can be repeated to give a continuous line. The technique is extremely useful if the beads are small and will not pass onto the yarn required for the crochet. However, if very small beads are used with a relatively thicker yarn, it will be found that the beads will not lie on the surface and will fall back onto the wrong side of the crochet.

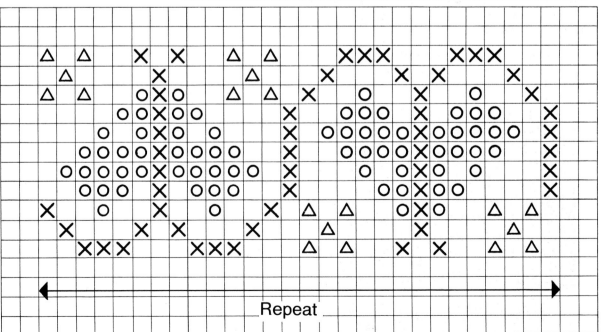

Repeat

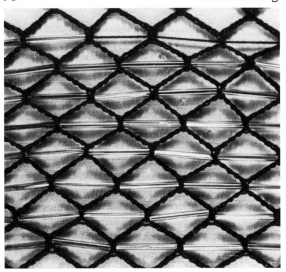

324 Beads placed into a fabric using a secondary yarn. The glass beads are 3 cm long and the open lace effect is achieved by working chain stitches between the beads. 1 double crochet stitch worked into the chain stitches below anchors the beads in place.

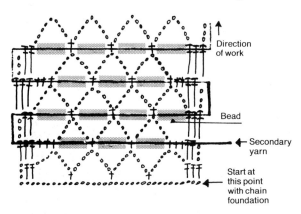

325 The method of working. The stitches are indicated by symbols. To make a wider fabric, add chain stitches in groups of 7 to the foundation length.

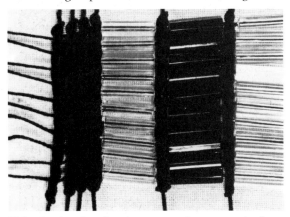

326 Beads placed onto a secondary yarn to form

warp threads in a bead loom. Weft threads to secure the beads in place are formed by working surface chain stitches across the warp threads. The beads in this sample are approximately 1.75 cm long, the warp threads should be a strong yarn and the surface chain stitches may be worked singly or in groups. It is important to secure the ends of these threads at the start and finish of each row. When the work is removed from the loom, all warp threads should be knotted.

Both these methods produce interesting beaded fabrics suitable for evening wear, accessories and trimmings.

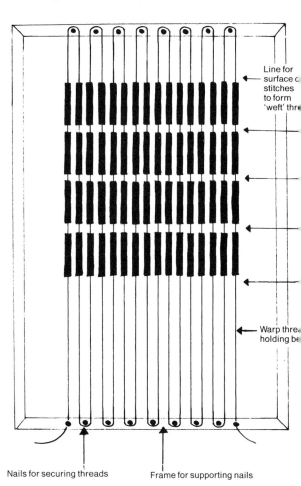

327 If a bead loom is not available, a substitute can be made using a small picture frame. The beads should fill the spaces between the warp threads so careful selection of beads and placing of the nails for securing warp threads is critical.

(c) **Beads sewn onto the crochet fabric**

Beads can be sewn onto a crochet fabric using a fine matching thread. It should, however, be remembered that crochet fabric is liable to move and stretch so any surface sewing should not be too restricting.

Crochet with stones

328 Stones polished in a domestic stone polishing machine form the main feature of this example. Yellow pebbles picked up from a beach make a golden

patterned stone when polished and various flat shapes are arranged together with some surface chain stitches and treble stitch coils. The stones are held in place by a trellis of treble stitches. Work a length of chain stitch and join to make a circle the same size as the stone to be held onto the fabric. Work 1 or 2 rows of double crochet followed by a row of trebles worked into every other double crochet stitch. Place the stone inside the crochet and sew the chain stitch foundation onto the fabric.

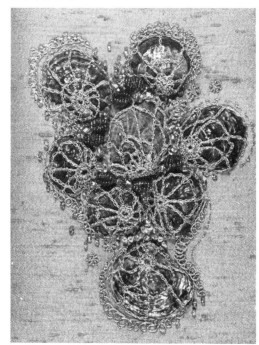

329 Shells and silver threads with a few tiny glass beads form this sample. Each shell is secured with a spider's web shape which is sewn onto the fabric. This is an example of working a spider's web, but each crochet shape is modified according to the size of shell. This is just a guide to start from:
Work 4 chain. Join with a slip stitch into the first chain stitch to form a circle.
Round 1 1 chain to count as 1 double crochet. 13 double crochet into the circle. Slip stitch into the first chain stitch.

Round 2
  4 chain, miss 1 double crochet, 1 treble into next double crochet.
  4 chain, miss 1 double crochet, 1 double treble into next double crochet.
  5 chain, miss 1 double crochet, 1 triple treble into next double crochet.
  5 chain, miss 1 double crochet, 1 quadruple treble into next double crochet.
  5 chain, miss 1 double crochet, 1 quadruple treble into next double crochet.
  4 chain, miss 1 double crochet, 1 triple treble into next double crochet.
  3 chain, 1 treble into next double crochet. 2 chain, 1 treble into next double crochet. 2 chain, slip stitch into second chain at start of round.

Round 3 5 chain. 1 treble into next treble. 5 chain, 1 double treble into next double treble. 7 chain, 1 triple treble into next triple treble. (8 chain, 1 quadruple treble into next quadruple treble) twice. 7 chain, 1 triple treble into next triple treble. 5 chain, 1 treble in next treble. 1 chain, 1 treble into next treble. 2 chain, slip stitch into second chain at start of round. Secure yarn.

These instructions are given only as a guide to help you start your own webs for securing shells. Much will depend on the size of the shells, and the thread and hook size being used.

Surface embroidery stitches and beads surround the shells on the sample.

Crochet to form shaped flowers using silver coloured wire

330 A fine silver thread worked in double crochet

and treble stitches form the petals and leaves of the rose. The shapes are edged with double crochet over wire which can be moulded and shaped to form a cupped petal.

A guide to working the petals: make a paper pattern of the required size of the petal. Trace round a real rose petal shape to give an outline. The crochet should lie within the paper shape. These instructions make a petal 5 cm × 5 cm. Begin the crochet with 5 chain.

Row 1   2 treble into 4th chain from hook. 1 treble in next chain. Turn work.

Row 2   3 chain to count as 1 treble. 1 treble into 4th stitch from hook. 2 treble in next 2 stitches. 1 treble into 3rd chain of turning chain. Turn work.

Row 3   4 chain to count as 1 treble and a 1-chain space. 1 treble into 5th stitch. *1 chain, 1 treble into next stitch*, repeat from * to * to end, placing last treble into 3rd chain of turning chain. Turn work.

Rows 4, 5, 6 and 7   Work in treble stitch, increasing 1 stitch at the beginning and end of each row. The number of rows and increases will depend on the petal size required. This is given a simple guide and variations can be included by working a chain stitch in place of a treble stitch to form spaces.

The leaves are worked along a centre line of chain stitches. Double crochet is worked along both sides of the chain, and wire can be placed inside the double crochet as you work along one side to give a firmness to the leaf. Further rows are worked around the centre shape working in trebles and 1-chain spaces. The stitches are decreased at both ends to give a tapered shape.

The coils are worked with double crochet over wire (see Chapter 8) crochet over cords. The completed crochet lengths are placed round and round a pencil to form into coils.

The crochet work is placed onto a silver quilted velvet background, the silver thread of the quilting echoing the silver threads of the crochet.

Crochet to hold Mica discs

Mica discs surrounded with crochet are shown in the following illustrations. The discs are reversible and the crochet is placed on both sides. The crochet could be used to form trimmings, insertions, centres for additional crochet or joined together to form a complete fabric.

331   Two spider's web shapes enclose the disc. The

web is made to form an irregular sequence of stitches and the reverse side is similar. The instructions on page 97 could be used as a starting point for these discs. The disc measures 4 cm in diameter, and the outer edges are joined together with chain stitches. The disc must be placed between the two crochet sides before the join is complete.

332   Discs measuring 5 cm in circumference sur-

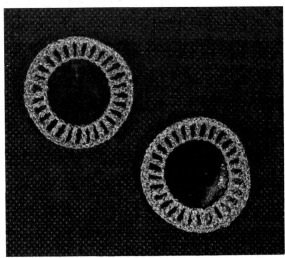

rounded by crochet in silver yarn. The method of working the surround is: work 28 chain stitches (ie a length shorter than the circumference of the disc). Join with a slip stitch to form a circle. Work 4 chain. 1 treble into 5th stitch from hook. 1 treble *1 chain, 1 treble into next chain stitch,* repeat from * to * to end of round. 1 chain, slip stitch into 3rd chain at start of round. Break off yarn. Work another circle in the same way. Place both circles together, and join outer edge with a row of double crochet, by inserting the hook under the stitches of both circles. Place disc between circles when one-half of the circle is joined together. Complete the double crochet stitches round the edge.

These instructions are given as a guide and the number of chain stitches to start the circular surrounds will vary according to the size of the discs, the type of yarn and hook size.

Crochet round polished stones to form pendants and rings

Polished stones of varying sizes may be completely surrounded with crochet using metallic threads to form pendants. A spider's web structure forms the base and extra long stitches, like a quadruple treble form the centre of the motif. These long stitches are worked by placing the yarn over the hook 8 times before the usual taking off of 2 loops each time.

333   The crochet is worked as previously explained; the stone is put in place before the crochet is drawn together to enclose the stone by 2 rounds of decreasing, ie work 1 stitch over every 2 stitches on both rounds. The stone is hung from a commercial gold chain.

333

Colour plate 11, facing page 93, shows a ring with a crochet surround made by the same technique.

All the techniques explained can be worked using fine copper wire, but the initial trial pieces are more easily worked using metallic type threads.

16 – Tunisian crochet

Tunisian crochet is also referred to as Crochet knitting, Railway crochet, Fool's crochet, Tricot stitch or Idiot stitch! The work is made by using a crochet hook which is much longer than the traditional crochet hook used for the standard type of work. Tunisian crochet hooks measure 35 cm and 30 cm in length and are available in sizes: 10 mm 9 mm 8 mm 7 mm 6 mm 5.5 mm in the longer length and 5 mm 4.5 mm 4 mm 3.5 mm 3 mm and 2.5 mm in the shorter length. There is another type of Tunisian crochet hook available, made in three pieces, each 20 cm long, which screw into each other and make one long hook. This is recommended for larger areas of work because the hook length governs the size of the finished crochet.

Tunisian crochet is different from traditional crochet in that a number of stitches are worked onto the hook – rather like knitting. A very firm and thick fabric is made which is suitable for many fashion garments and accessories. This chapter covers the basic Tunisian crochet techniques together with the methods for increasing and decreasing, textured stitches and stitches using two colours. The basic stitch makes a very suitable base fabric for additional surface stitchery, either worked with a crochet hook or a sewing needle. Tunisian crochet is not turned at the end of each row. This technique produces a definite right and wrong side to the fabric. The right side of the fabric faces you throughout the working of the stitches. Tunisian crochet is worked in pairs of rows:

(a)   The first row is worked from right to left, placing the stitches onto the hook – sometimes referred to as the casting on row, or the 'pick up' row.

(b)   The second row is worked from left to right which is a casting off of the stitches from the hook – sometimes known as the 'casting off' row.

A foundation chain length must be worked before the initial casting on row.

Method of working the basic Tunisian crochet stitch

Normally referred to as tricot stitch.
Make a chain length – eg 20 stitches.
334 and 335   **Row 1**   Insert hook into second chain

from hook, yarn over hook and draw through yarn (334). *Insert hook into next chain, yarn over hook and draw through yarn*, repeat from * to * to end of chain length (335). There will be 20 stitches on the hook, ie the number of chain stitches for the foundation chain length determines exactly the number of stitches on the hook at the end of the first row.

336–338   **Row 2**   Yarn over hook (336) and draw yarn through the first 2 loops on hook (337). *Yarn over hook and draw yarn through next 2 loops on hook,* repeat from * to * to end of row. There will be 1 loop only left on the hook (338).

This increase is best worked 1 or 2 stitches inside the first and last stitches in order to avoid uneven edges to the work.

342   1 increased stitch on the edges of the fabric.

343   1 increased stitch over 5 pairs of Tunisian crochet rows to give shaping in mid-row.

339 and 340 Row 3 Insert hook under second vertical loop on the front of fabric of previous row. Yarn over hook and draw through yarn (339).
Insert hook under next vertical loop on fabric surface (340) yarn over hook and draw through yarn, repeat from * to * to end of row. There should be 20 stitches on hook.
Row 4 Repeat row 2.
Rows 3 and 4 form the pair of rows for tricot stitch.

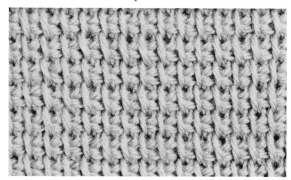

341   Tricot stitch sample

Shaping in Tunisian crochet

Work in Tunisian crochet can be shaped in the same manner as for traditional crochet. Stitches can be increased and decreased on the edges of the work or in the process of working a row.
Increasing   To increase 1 stitch on the edges of your work or in the middle of a row, work the increase on the 'pick up' row. Work 1 extra pick up stitch between the vertical loops, ie, insert the hook under the horizontal loop lying between the vertical loops.

To increase more than 1 stitch at the start of a row, work the extra chain stitches required before starting the pick up row. Work along the extra stitches before the main part of the row. To increase more than 1 stitch at the end of the row, complete the pick up row, then take a spare piece of yarn and work the required extra chain stitches. Secure to last stitch of previous row, and continue the pick up row over the extra chain stitches.
Decreasing   Single decreased stitches on the sides of your work or in the middle of a row are worked by inserting the hook under 2 vertical loops on the pick up row instead of the 1 loop. Decreased stitches can be worked at any required position.

344   1 decreased stitch on the sides – second stitch in from the edges.

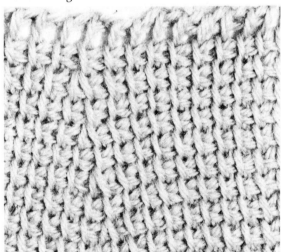

345   1 decreased stitch worked over 4 pairs of rows to give shaping in the middle of a row.

Decreasing more than 1 stitch at the start of a row requires slip stitching over the required number of horizontal loops which lie between the vertical loops at the start of the pick up row. To decrease more than 1 stitch at the end of a row, work the pick up row to the marked position for the decrease to start, then continue with the cast off row.

To achieve a more textured effect using the Tunisian technique, the position for the hook insertion on the pick up row can be changed. By altering the position of the hook insertion many alterations are possible. Most patterns begin by working the first 2 rows of the basic stitch, that is the pick up row and the cast off row. Also, for most patterns the cast off row remains unchanged. All Tunisian crochet work is best tried out for the first time using a DK yarn and a 5.00 ISR Tunisian Crochet hook.

346   Make a chain length multiple of 3 + 2. Work the first 2 rows as for the basic Tunisian crochet.
Row 3   Miss the first vertical loop, *place yarn over hook from front to back fairly loosely, (insert hook into next vertical loop, yarn over hook and draw through yarn) 3 times, – 5 loops on hook. Take 4th loop back and pass over 3 loops,* repeat from * to * to last stitch. Pick up 1 stitch from last vertical loop.
Row 4   Work the normal cast off row.
Rows 3 and 4 form this pattern.

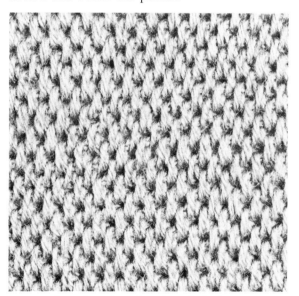

347   Make a chain length and work the first 2 rows as for basic Tunisian crochet.
Row 3   Work as for basic stitch inserting the hook under the complete chain stitch between the vertical loops. Care should be taken not to 'loose' stitches when working this row and a stitch count is recommended at the end of the row.
Row 4   Work the normal cast off row.
Rows 3 and 4 form this pattern.

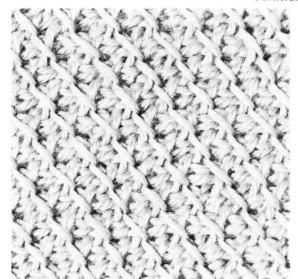

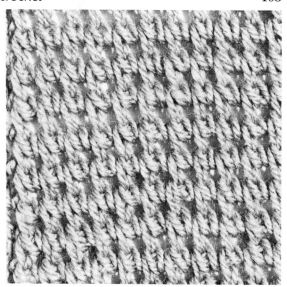

348   Make a chain length multiple of 2. Work the first 2 rows as for the basic Tunisian crochet.
Row 3   Miss first vertical loop. *Insert hook under next 2 vertical loops, yarn over hook and draw through yarn, insert hook under the first of these 2 loops, yarn over hook and draw through yarn,* repeat from * to * to last stitch. Pick up 1 stitch from last vertical loop.
Row 4   Work the normal cast off row.
Rows 3 and 4 form this pattern.

349   'Stocking stitch'. Make a chain length and work the first 2 rows as for the basic Tunisian crochet.
Row 3   Work as for the basic Tunisian crochet stitch but insert the hook right through the crochet from front to back of work. The hook is placed under the complete chain stitch and on the right hand side of the vertical loop normally used on the pick up row. This fabric is very thick and firm, and tends to curl more than the other types of Tunisian crochet fabrics.
Row 4   Work the normal cast off row. Rows 3 and 4 from this pattern.

350   Make a chain length and work the first 2 rows as for basic Tunisian crochet.
Row 3   *Insert hook under the complete chain stitch between next 2 vertical loops, yarn over hook and draw through yarn. Insert hook under next single vertical loop, yarn over hook and draw yarn through and through 1 loop on hook,* repeat from * to * to end of row.
Row 4   Work the normal cast off row.

   Many of the Tunisian crochet fabrics make ideal textures for floor rugs if made with a No. 8.00 hook and string. (The string should be between 4–6 mm in diameter). Obviously the hook length determines the width of the fabric made, but strips can be sewn together for wider floor coverings. Squares in Tunisian crochet joined together with opposing line effects also make attractive rugs, similar in appearance to the traditional rush squares.

Tunisian crochet using two colours of yarn

351   A striped fabric using two colours of yarn. Many combinations of stitches and colours could be substituted for the ones given below.

With colour A, work 6 rows in the basic Tunisian crochet stitch over a foundation chain length.

Join in colour B, and work 2 chain, *yarn over hook and insert hook between next 2 vertical loops, yarn over hook and draw through yarn extending loop to the same height of the chain stitch,* repeat from * to * to end of row.

The next row is the cast off row and should be worked: yarn over hook and draw through 2 loops, *yarn over hook and draw through 3 loops*, repeat from * to * to end of row.

Colour A. On the next pick up row, insert hook under the horizontal loop at the back of the work for each stitch. It is important to make a stitch count at the end of this row, as stitches can be 'lost'.

Several rows in basic Tunisian crochet may be worked before working another stripe in colour B. The yarn need not be cut at the end of each stripe but carried upwards at the side of your work.

352 Tunisian crochet with bobbles in another colour.

This very textured fabric can be worked in one colour throughout or with one colour for the background and one or more different colours for the bobbles. The background fabric is worked in the basic Tunisian crochet stitch and the bobbles can be made at whatever intervals your design calls for.

To work a bobble in Tunisian crochet

Work along the pick up row until the position is reached for the bobble. Leave working yarn of main colour behind work. Insert hook under the next vertical loop and draw through yarn of contrasting colour. Using the contrast colour (place yarn over hook, insert hook under vertical loop below last hook insertion – 2 or more rows down – depending on the size of the bobble required – yarn over hook and draw through yarn extending loop on hook to required length) 4 times. Yarn over hook and draw through all loops on hook in contrast colour. Leave contrast yarn to the back of work and continue in basic stitch in main colour yarn to end of row. If the bobbles are fairly close together, the yarn can be carried behind the work.

Surface stitchery can be applied to Tunisian crochet fabric using many of the stitches illustrated in figure 272, page 77. Threading ribbon and contrasting yarns under the vertical loops also gives scope for surface decoration.

Most Tunisian crochet tends to curl when finished, so it should be noted that careful pinning, blocking and pressing is very necessary (see page 119).

17 – Working methods

Selecting your first crochet project

There are five different ways to plan and work a crochet project. Each method has its own appeal, depending on the skill and experience of the worker.

    (a) Select and use a commercial crochet pattern.
    (b) Use the outline of a commercial paper pattern for a fashion garment.
    (c) Use the outline of an existing garment.
    (d) Use a graph pattern as illustrated.
    (e) Spontaneous crochet – no initial pattern.

(a) Using a commercial crochet pattern

Many beginners select a commercial crochet pattern for their first project. These designs and instructions are usually well prepared and use the yarns most suited to the garment. You should always buy the stated yarn, the correct amount of the same dye batch, and work your tension piece before starting work. The tension refers to the closeness of each stitch in your work to the next and the correct tension is imperative for a garment which must be of a definite size. If, however, you decide to make an article such as a cushion or shawl the tension is not so critical.

To test your tension Use the stated yarn and hook size. Work a reasonable sized piece of crochet fabric in the selected pattern stitch. The tension piece should be worked over approximately 20–30 stitches for the foundation chain and 25 rows should follow. This is a worthwhile preparation and it is helpful for whatever type of work is to be undertaken. These samples to test tension should be clearly labelled and marked with the yarn and hook used. When the sample is complete, place your work on a flat surface such as an ironing board and pin down at the corners. The crochet should lie quite flat. Using a measure or ruler, place glass headed pins on the crochet at 5 cm intervals, both vertically (to count the rows) and horizontally (to count the stitches).

353   A tension of 7 rows to 5 cm in double crochet stitch using a 5.00 ISR hook and a chunky yarn.

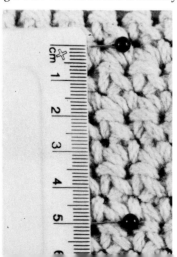

354   A tension of 5 double crochet to 5 cm using a 5.00 ISR crochet hook and chunky yarn.

The method for testing tension is the same for all crochet stitch patterns. It is always worthwhile making these test pieces a good size because the test measure should be taken in the centre of the work. If there is any doubt, that is if part of a stitch or row lies in the test measurement, try measuring over a 10 cm square or one even larger. This gives a more realistic guide. Always write the tension count onto the label of your sample piece. These pieces make useful reference information for future work.

Problems with tension If it is imperative to have an article of an exact size, your tension must be the *same* as that quoted. Therefore, if you have too many stitches and too many rows in the sample, the tension is too tight and you should change to a larger hook size. If you have too few stitches and rows, the tension is too loose and you should use a smaller hook size.

    It will be noted, sometimes, that while working these test samples, the foundation chain may curl causing your work to curve. This is due to the fact that your chain is too tight, and a larger hook size used only for the foundation chain helps to overcome this defect.

    For a foundation chain requiring many stitches, place markers (safety pins or pieces of contrasting yarn) at 20-stitch intervals to facilitate accurate counting.

Brackets (. . . . .) Brackets will appear in commercial crochet patterns and are used to save repeating instructions in full each time they are to be worked. Usually brackets are followed by a number which indicates the number of times the information within the brackets is to be worked. Therefore, if you read (1 chain, miss 1 stitch, 1 treble in next 2 stitches) 8 times – you work the instructions exactly 8 times, before reading the next step. Sometimes brackets can be used to enclose instructions worked into one particular position. For example, (1 double crochet, 1 half treble, 1 treble, 2 chain, 1 treble, 1 half treble, 1 double crochet) into next space. This would indicate that all the instructions within the brackets would be worked into the *same* position.

Star/asterisk *. . . . . . .* Two stars contain more information than brackets and the information between the ** should be repeated until:

(i)   the end of the row or round or

(ii)   until the last stitch, when the instructions will go on to say, 1 treble (or whatever) in last stitch.

It is always worthwhile to read right through the instructions for the given row, to see where the repeats finish. Sometimes a number is given, ie repeat from * to * 10 more times. You would therefore work the instructions within the ** 11 times in total.

When reading commercial patterns it is advisable to underline the size you are working towards, the various sizes being given in brackets after the smallest size. This primary reading through of the written instructions helps to give you an overall outline of the shape, the number of pieces to be made and an idea of the shaping.

All commercial patterns expect you to work from right to left, turning your work at the end of each row; if the work is not to be turned, this is stated. The yarn is never broken or changed unless stated.

Always work into each consecutive stitch of the previous row, unless told to miss 1 stitch, remembering that *all* crochet stitches are counted as 1 *stitch*, even 1 chain stitch.

(b)   Crochet worked to the outline of a commercial paper pattern for a fashion garment

355   Coat made from the paper pattern of a Tibetan

panel coat prepared by 'Folkwear' in their Ethnic Pattern range, No. 118. It is available in three sizes, small 6–8, medium 10–12 and large 14–16–18. (See also colour plate 1, facing page 92). This pattern was selected for a base pattern shape for crochet textures. Working from a commercial pattern is suitable for someone wishing to be a little more creative, and leaves room for selecting your own yarns and stitch patterns. It is always advisable to choose the best yarns you can afford, because you will be putting a great deal of time and thought into the making of the garment. It is wise to make something which will last well.

When the paper pattern is chosen, it should be made up in calico. The calico outfit is known as a toile and can be tried on to test the fit. Garments without darts are easier than garments with darts so for first attempts select a dartless pattern. Patterns suggested for stretch fabric are always very suitable for crochet. Remember that crochet garments can stretch and drop. The toile should therefore not be too loose and long. Adjust the toile if necessary, and when satisfied with the fit, undo the seams and use the calico pieces for your guide to the crochet work.

Method of working crochet to a paper pattern shape (or a calico toile shape)

1   Make sure the seamline is clearly marked on the pattern (356).

2   Decide on the hook, yarn, and stitch pattern to be used. Work a test sample using a 25 gm ball of yarn (356).

3   Note the tension count.

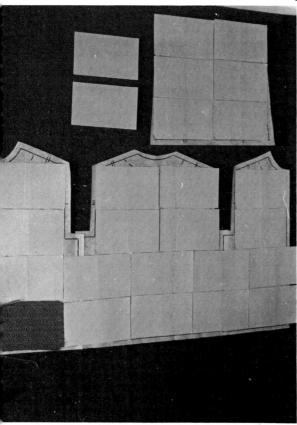

your work or in the middle of a row – this can cause problems if working to a definite stitch pattern. Lay the crochet over the calico shape at least every other row in order to check the size.

Write down exactly what you do, ie the stitch number, where you increase or decrease, etc. This is most useful when working two or more pattern pieces of the same shape. Do remember, however, that the left-hand side and right-hand side of a garment, such as a cardigan, need to be worked in reverse order for the second side.

9 On completion of the crochet for all the given pattern pieces, block, press and sew together to finish garment. (Instructions for blocking – see page 119). Work any edging if required.

Note If there are darts on your paper pattern, these can be worked open, ie divide your crochet when you reach the position of the dart and continue working to the shape on one side of the dart, until you reach the top. Break off the yarn and work along the second side of the dart to the shape required until the top is reached. Work along the original crochet to make one continuous line of crochet. Care must be taken that the joining row is worked in the correct direction. Make sure, therefore, that the number of rows on each side of the dart are exactly the same. This also facilitates the sewing up of the dart.

(c) Crochet worked to the outline of an existing garment

It is also possible to take a pattern from an existing garment which you feel suits you and fits well. This should be fairly basic in shape such as a skirt or sleeveless jerkin. To make an outline, lay the skirt very flat onto a large sheet of brown paper, with the centre front and centre back placed in the centre. Draw round the outside of the fabric to give an outline for your crochet. If the garment fits you comfortably, your paper pattern should not require testing by making a toile shape. Use the brown paper shape exactly – no seam or hem allowances will be included. Follow the instructions on pages 106 and 107 to complete your garment.

(d) Crochet worked to one of the graph designs illustrated

All the designs shown in this book, except the Tibetan coat, have been worked from original drawings. Paper patterns were made by established drafting techniques,[6] and calico toiles were made and fitted. The crochet was then worked to the toile pattern as explained previously. All the outline shapes for the designs are given in graph form and would fit the average size figure of 88 cm to 92 cm bust. *No seam allowances are shown*, therefore if a toile pattern is required, a seam allowance of 1.5 cm should be given to allow for seaming. To make your own pattern from these graphs, let 1 square equal 1 cm. Make a toile from your paper pattern and check for style and fit.

These are basic and simple designs and if you wish to make them smaller or larger additional amounts, or reductions, can usually be made on the seamlines.

4 357 Make several oblongs of paper the same size as the crochet sample, and lay on the complete calico pattern. Do not extend over the seam allowances and hems. This will give you an estimate of the required amount of yarn needed for the garment. This method is applicable to all designs where an estimate is required. Remember to allow for both sleeves. The amount required for this design is 30 balls of 25 gm.

5 Decide on the direction of the crochet, ie north to south, or east to west. Mark the direction on the calico. Mark the positions for starting the crochet foundation for each pattern piece.

6 Measure the length of the pattern piece which will form your starting point.

7 Calculate the number of stitches required to start the pattern piece: if the tension count gave 8 stitches to 10 cm and the measurement of your starting point on the calico toile is 50 cm you would need: $\frac{50}{10} \times 8 = 40$ stitches.

Do not be misled by the length of your foundation chain; this will not give an accurate indication of the length it will be when complete. Go on working the required stitch pattern for several rows before checking the crochet against the calico shape.

8 Work to your calico shape. Your crochet should lie within the fitting line (the seamline of the commercial pattern) and normally the hem allowance would not be included in your crochet.

Check for any necessary shaping, ie increasing or decreasing. This may be carried out on the sides of

This should be carried out at the fitting stage of the toile.

It is important to note the fold line on your pattern, eg for centre back and centre front. These fold lines should be placed to a fold on the calico for cutting out the complete pattern piece. If you are satisfied with the toile, unpick the seams and use the shape for the outline of your crochet.

The arrows on the graph patterns indicate the starting position for each piece. The dotted lines indicate the border trimmings and edgings worked after the main part of the crochet has been completed. Therefore, the main crochet work should finish on the dotted lines. Wedge-shaped marks indicate seams to be joined together.

All crochet work should lie within the seam allowance if shown on your pattern. Some working notes on the graph designs given may help you while working these garments.

For all the designs shown, the yarn amount used is quoted, but this will only apply if you use the same stitch with the same hook and the yarn quoted. For different crochet stitches you should work a test sample using one ball of yarn chosen, and calculate the amount of yarn required as shown in figure 357. The yarn used for the sample should be the *same* type, but need not be the colour chosen. When the amount required is known the full amount can be purchased in the same dye lot of the colour you have chosen.

358   A blouson top and skirt. The top requires 28 balls of Paton's DK yarn in 25 gm balls. Oddments of contrasting colours are needed for the stripes. The crochet stitch is illustrated in figure 97, page 30. A 4.50 ISR crochet hook gives a firm tension.

The skirt requires 35 balls of Paton's DK yarn in 25 gm balls and one ball of a contrasting yarn for the decorative seaming. The crochet stitch is treble and double crochet worked in alternate rows. A 4.50 ISR crochet hook is recommended.

Key to graph pattern outlines

Position for starting crochet   ←

Balance marks, ie the position of
seams to be placed and joined together   ◄

Shoulder point   ◆

Underarm position   ◆

Centre of pattern piece.
This line should be
placed to a fold
of the fabric when
cutting fabric for toile

Position for working
border trimmings when the
main garment areas
are completed

The graph lines indicate the grain of the calico when cutting the fabric for making the toile. The straight of grain should run from shoulder to hem, ie the warp.

No seam allowances are indicated.

1 graph square represents 1 centimetre.

Figure 359 shows the pattern pieces for the top. The back and front are the same shape – two pieces to be made. The sleeve is the same for both sides – two should be made. Note the underarm position on the bodice section, the shoulder point on the sleeve and the neck opening. Draw strings are placed through alternate stitches around wrist and waistline.

Figure 360 shows the three pattern pieces for the skirt. The centre panel forms the centre back section and the centre front section. The four side panels complete the skirt – each piece should be made twice. Six sections should be made in total. It is advisable to start the crochet from the waist line, and any hem adjustment in length can be easily and quickly made at this position. If the crochet stitch pattern chosen has a right and wrong side in appearance, it is imperative that the left and right side panels are mirror images. Elastic is placed along the waistline of the skirt (figure 381).

Right, above
359   Outline pattern for the blouson top in 358

Right, below
360   Outline for the skirt in 358.

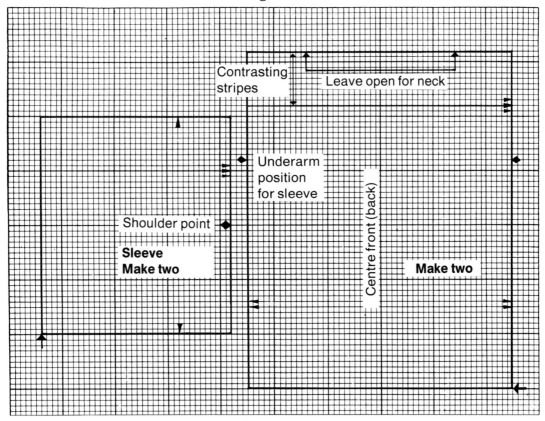

Contrasting stripes

Leave open for neck

Underarm position for sleeve

Centre front (back)

Shoulder point

Sleeve
Make two

Make two

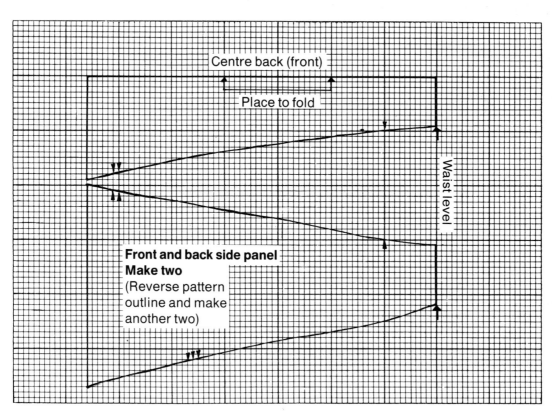

Centre back (front)

Place to fold

Waist level

Front and back side panel
Make two
(Reverse pattern
outline and make
another two)

361 A large shawl made in stripes requiring 31 balls of 25 gm wool in contrasting shades. The crochet stitch is worked in trebles and chain stitches using a 4.50 ISR crochet hook and DK yarn.

362 The outline shape for making the shawl – the fringe is not included in the measurements. Crochet can be worked from the narrow edge working upwards. Note the 30 cm slit for the arms – the shawl is worn doubled. Two rows of additional crochet stitches are worked all round the outside edge before applying the fringe. This will make a good line over the shaped edging.

363 A Chanel type cardigan. 30 balls of Patons *Trident* DK yarn in 25 gm balls are required for this cardigan. A No. 5.00 ISR crochet hook is recommended and the stitch is a variation on the half treble: 1 row worked in half treble throughout; the second row reads – 1 chain to count as 1 double crochet, 1 double crochet into 3rd stitch from hook. *1 half treble placing hook through space behind last double crochet worked. Miss 1 stitch of previous row. 1 double crochet into next stitch*, repeat from * to * to end of row working last double crochet into the turning chain. Turn work. This stitch pattern gives a very striped textured effect and both sides of the crochet fabric are different.

Figure 364 shows the complete paper pattern for the cardigan. The crochet is worked between the dotted lines on the outer edge of the pattern. A border line of crochet is worked over cords as explained in Chapter 8. Note the position of the shoulder point on the sleeve.

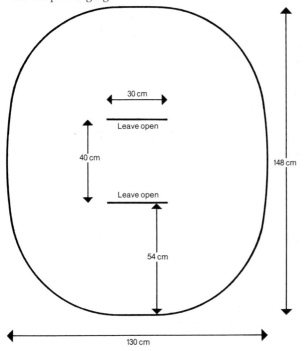

364 Outline pattern for the Chanel jacket in 363
(a) Front and back
(b) Sleeve

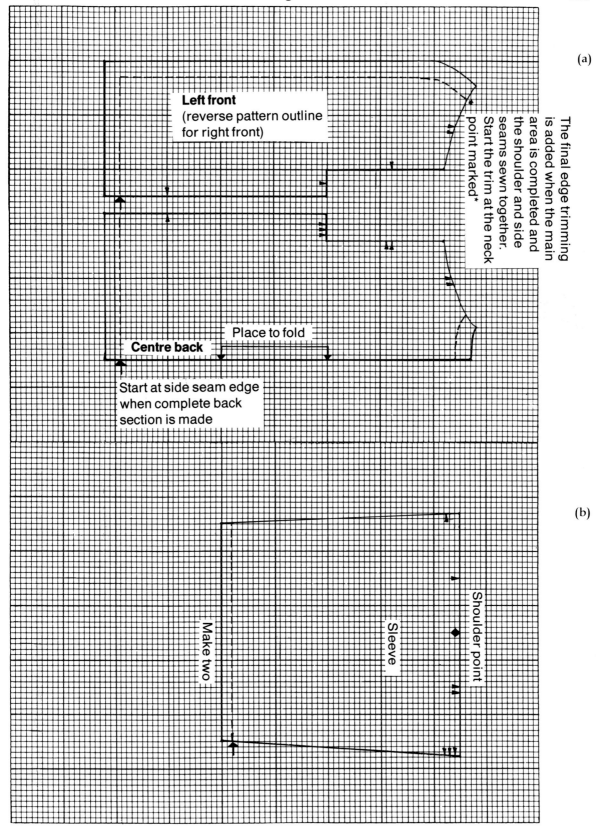

(a)

Left front
(reverse pattern outline
for right front)

The final edge trimming
is added when the main
area is completed and
the shoulder and side
seams sewn together.
Start the trim at the neck
point marked*

Place to fold

Centre back

Start at side seam edge
when complete back
section is made

(b)

Make two

Sleeve

Shoulder point

365   A mid-calf length dress made in Patons *Fiona Banff* brown yarn with a contrasting yarn in Patons *Kismet* buttermilk shade used for the seams. 17 balls of 50 gm are required for this dress, using a No. 3.50 ISR crochet hook. The stitch pattern is 1 row treble and 1 row double crochet.

Figure 366 shows the pattern pieces for the dress. The back and front are almost the same shape, the back is slightly higher at the neck line. Two side panels are required – both alike, and two sleeves. *Note*   Balance marks nos. 1 and 2 refer to the fitting line on the front sleeve; nos. 3 and 4 refer to the fitting line on the back sleeve. The crochet can be started from either the top or the hem. The same comments apply as for the skirt on page 108.

Right
366   Outline pattern for the dress in 365

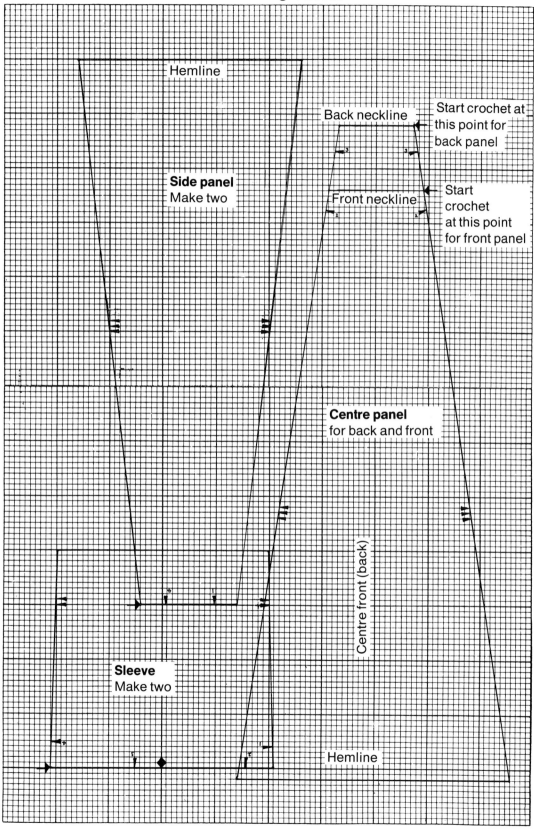

Hemline

Back neckline

Start crochet at this point for back panel

Side panel
Make two

Front neckline

Start crochet at this point for front panel

Centre panel
for back and front

Centre front (back)

Sleeve
Make two

Hemline

367   A two piece made in Twilley's *Capricorn* bulky knitting yarn. Five balls (100 gm) are required for the top, and 4 balls (100 gm) for the skirt. An open stitch using trebles and chains forms the stitch pattern. A 7.00 ISR crochet hook is recommended. The sleeve of the top introduces various shades of Twilley's *Lystwist* using a No. 3.00 ISR crochet hook.

Figures 368 and 369 show the pattern pieces for the two piece. The top is worked from wrist to wrist within the dotted lines. Additional rows of crochet complete the wrist, neck opening and peplum at the waist. A draw string gathers the top into the waistline. The skirt can be worked in continuous rounds, increasing to give the shaping over the hip line.

Elastic is placed along the waistline of the skirt (figure 381) and through the wristline.

Right, above
368   Outline pattern for the top in 367

Right, below
369   Outline pattern for the skirt in 367

Batsford Book Information Service

NAME _____

ADDRESS _____

_____

_____ POST CODE _____

Please fill in your NAME and ADDRESS together with the TITLE of this book if you wish to receive further information on Batsford books. (If you have sent us a card already, please pass this on to a friend).

TITLE OF BOOK _____

 B.T. BATSFORD LTD
4 Fitzhardinge Street, London W1H 0AH

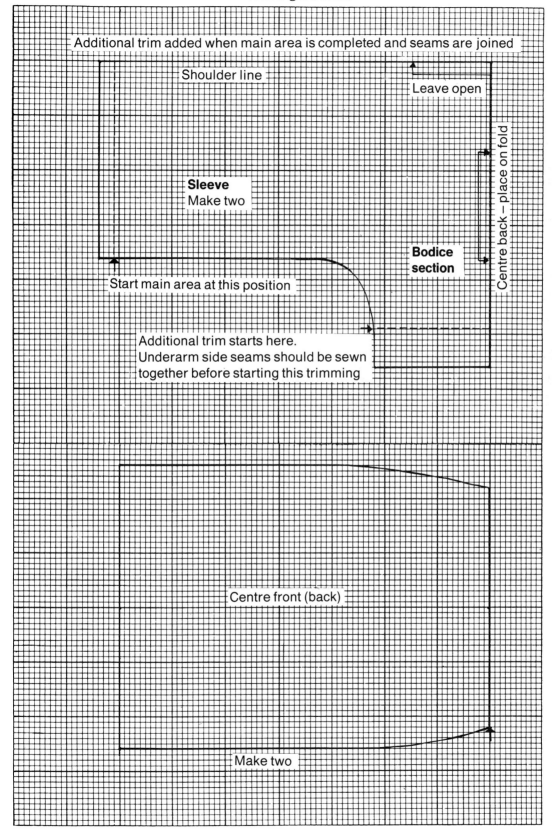

Additional trim added when main area is completed and seams are joined

Shoulder line

Leave open

Centre back – place on fold

Sleeve
Make two

Bodice section

Start main area at this position

Additional trim starts here.
Underarm side seams should be sewn
together before starting this trimming

Centre front (back)

Make two

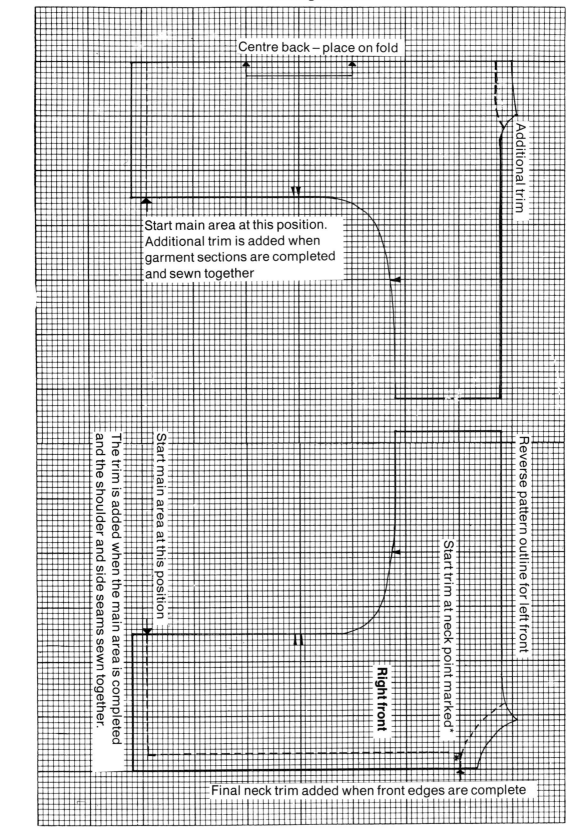

Centre back – place on fold

Additional trim

Start main area at this position.
Additional trim is added when
garment sections are completed
and sewn together

Reverse pattern outline for left front

Start main area at this position

The trim is added when the main area is completed
and the shoulder and side seams sewn together.

Start trim at neck point marked*

Right front

Final neck trim added when front edges are complete

Left

370 Outline pattern for the patchwork jacket in 00 Figure 370 shows the two pattern pieces for a simple jacket. The patchwork pieces are placed together to fill the area between the dotted lines, and a plain double crochet border finishes the edges of the jacket. The jacket requires 28 balls (25 gm) in ten different shades of Paton's *Trident* 4-ply yarn. A 3.50 ISR crochet hook is recommended to give a very close stitch.

Figure 371 shows the pattern outline for the bolero shown in colour plate 4, between pages 92/3.

372 The complete pattern (seam allowances are shown as a calico toile was tested for this bolero), and free crochet being tested for size against the paper pattern. The crochet is worked in various directions using a variety of stitches, leather pieces, and yarns.

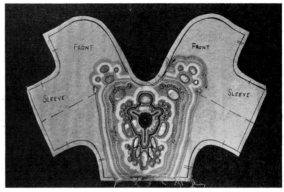

372

Only the underarm seam requires sewing together when the crochet is complete.

Method of working a crochet design to a circular hat shape The following diagram gives a basic hat shape made up in six sections. If the head size is too large, reduce the shape on each side by one-twelfth of the amount to be reduced. Also check the overall measurement for depth of each section.

371

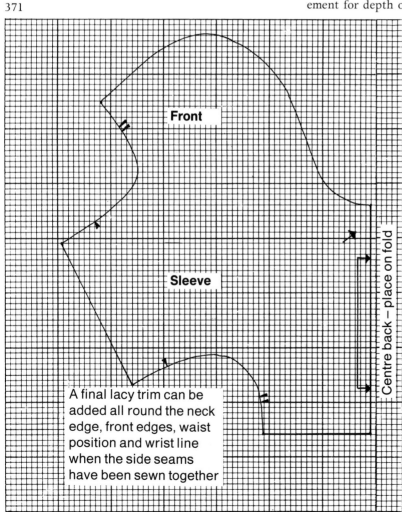

Front

Sleeve

Centre back – place on fold

A final lacy trim can be added all round the neck edge, front edges, waist position and wrist line when the side seams have been sewn together

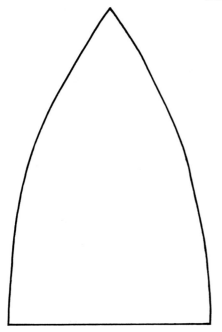

373 Pattern for a six-section hat shape. The pattern should have a 10 cm base, height 15 cm – head fitting 60 cm. No seam allowances are indicated.

Work a trial sample to test your crochet stitches etc, working to the shape of one section. You can begin either at the tip or the base of the section, increasing if you start at the tip, decreasing if you start at the base on both sides to give the required shape. Write down exactly when you increase or decrease and how many rows you work between each increase or decrease row. Keep the work slightly inside the paper shape as some stretching makes the hat a closer and better fit. It is really advisable to start at the tip and work towards the base as further crochet can then be easily added for a brim. To work the complete hat shape, work in circles (complete, not spirals) working each row of the trial sample six times consecutively. Check the final measurement with the calculations given in Chapter 13 for circular work.

Brims can be added by working extra crochet onto the head line of the hat shape, testing every row for style. Increased stitches will be required to form the brim.

(e) Spontaneous crochet work

Some crochet work can be produced by sketching an outline of a design, eg a jerkin top, leg warmers, simply indicating the colour and/or texture required. The crochet can then be worked freely, by holding the work against a figure to check size and overall appeal.

It must be stressed that this is a very 'free' way of working and is only suitable for some people and some designs.

Edgings and finishes to crochet work

The final appearance of most crochet is improved by a finishing crochet edging which is worked as an addition. There are several techniques shown in this book:

(a)   Double crochet.
(b)   Double crochet worked in reverse.
(c)   Frilled edgings.
(d)   Chain stitch.

(a)   Double crochet   When working double crochet round any edge, always place the hook under 2 loops, not 1, and not more than 2. If the hook is placed under 3 loops, a small hole is made and forms an untidy join. Mark the edge of the crochet with safety pins at 5 cm intervals and then refer back to your test sample for the stitch count. Count the number of double crochet stitches worked over a 5 cm measurement. Work the same number of double crochet stitches for your edging between each pin mark. If you have no sample in double crochet, it is well worth making one to avoid a fluted edge or an edge which is too short and will cause dragging. Sometimes a length of yarn can be placed along the double crochet row, and the stitches are then worked over this yarn (see page 64). This will help to control the edge and makes a very pleasing ribbed texture. It will also help to prevent the garment edge stretching and dropping during wear. Several rows of double crochet can be used for an edging, and several thicknesses of yarn can be introduced to give a thick corded effect.

(b)   Double crochet worked in reverse   This was explained in Chapter 5, page 48. The markers should be placed as for the previous method.

(c)   Frilled edging   See the bolero in colour plate 4, between pages 92/3, which shows a frilled edging worked into the main crochet fabric. A finer cotton thread with hook of appropriate size produces a more lace-like fabric. The stitches used are treble, with 1-chain spaces between. On every row, increased stitches are worked to produce the frilling. Various designs can be made using the increasing technique. The lace has a richer effect if used double.

(d)   Chain stitching as an edging   The Aran style Tibetan coat in colour plate 1, facing page 92 features a chained line of stitching along the outside edge of the centre front and hemline. This is achieved by working a line of surface chain stitch on the very outer edge of the crochet fabric.

Joining yarn and sewing in the ends

Knots for joining are best avoided because an uneven lump will be made. Always try to join in a new yarn length at the start of a row. The ends can then be sewn into the seams when they are sewn together. If a join is required during the work of a row, tie a very loose knot while working the crochet. When the piece of crochet is finished, undo the knot and darn in the cut ends on the wrong side of the fabric.

If using a contrasting coloured yarn, the new colour should be joined into your work during the making of the last stitch in the main colour (see figure 205, page 54). The cut end may be darned into the wrong side of the fabric. If a permanent knot is required, eg when securing the hairpin circles in Chapter 14, an overhand knot should be made, and it will stay in place without slipping.

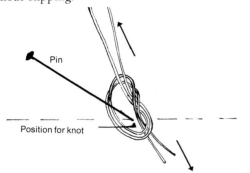

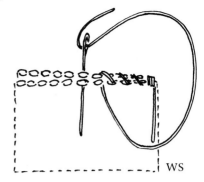

(a)

374 Overhand knot. Note the position of the pin to place the knot where required.

Blocking and pressing

This is a process to improve the appearance of a piece of work before each piece is sewn together. It is most important and care should be taken to avoid over working and pressing your crochet.

A large flat surface such as a kitchen table or working surface is required. This should be well protected with several thicknesses of blankets and covered with a clean towel. Make sure all the thicknesses of material are quite smooth and flat. Lay your calico or paper pattern onto the towel and place a line of pins all round the edge at 5 cm intervals approximately. Remove the pattern piece. Place the right side of the crochet piece onto the towel and pin along the edges matching the outline shape on the towel. Cover the crochet with a damp cotton towel and very gently press the work with the iron set on the correct heat setting for the yarn content. Always check the yarn on the wrapper of the ball. Avoid pushing the iron while pressing your work: use an up and down movement. Leave the work until completely dry, which may take several hours. Join all seams. Some further light pressing may be used on the seamlines.

Joining pieces of crochet work together

All work should be blocked and pressed before joining together.

There are five methods of joining crochet given in this chapter:

(a) Sewing – over sewing or 'draw' stitch.
(b) Surface chain stitch.
(c) Double crochet.
(d) Braid cord stitch.
(e) Chain stitches.

(a) Sewing

375 (a) The method of over sewing. The right sides of the fabric are placed together (safety pins may be used to hold them in place). Always match together stripes in colour and texture. If two different colours are used in the crochet for a seam length of more than 5 cm, the sewing thread should be changed to match each piece. Care should be taken to secure firmly the

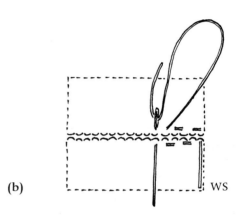

(b)

start and finish of each seam. A short length of yarn is left loose at the start of a seam, and this piece should be threaded back into the seam when finished.

375 (b) The draw stitch method gives a slightly flatter seam. Again pin the crochet fabric together matching rows, before starting to work the draw stitch. This method is very suitable for thick fabrics. Some people use the back stitch method, leaving a seam allowance on their work. This can leave a bumpy line and is difficult to press flat.

(b) Surface chain stitch

Place the two pieces of fabric to be joined with wrong sides together. Place a slip loop on the hook and, starting at beginning of seamline, *insert hook under both loops of next stitch on both pieces. Yarn over hook and draw yarn through work and through loop on hook*, repeat from * to * to end of seam. This produces a slightly raised chain line along the seam.

(c) Double crochet

Hold the work as for (b) and starting at beginning of seamline place a slip loop on the hook, and *insert hook under both loops of next stitch on both pieces. Yarn over hook and draw yarn through work, yarn over hook and draw yarn through both loops on hook*, repeat from * to * to end of seam. This produces an attractive raised joined seamline.

(d) Braid cord stitch

The skirt in figure 358 illustrates the panel seams joined

by this method. Double crochet is worked on the outer edge of each crochet piece prior to the working of the cord stitch. The cord stitch is worked by placing the hook through both loops on both pieces of crochet working from the right side. Cord stitch is explained in detail on page 31.

(e) Chain stitches

This is a useful method for joining work in open fabrics or for joining squares. Work along one edge by making a series of chained loops. There should be about 5 chains in each loop depending on the design. Complete one edge working on the right side. Join yarn onto a second edge, and work 2 chain. Insert hook into chained loop on adjacent edge, draw yarn through chained loop and through loop on hook, work 2 chain and continue along edge working joins with chained loops as required. The hairpin motifs in colour plate 3, between pages 92/3 are joined by this method.

Undoing work

Crochet is quick to undo and should therefore be securely finished at all times. However, if it is necessary to undo work, this is quite simple to do. All yarn should be washed before working again to remove crinkles in the yarn. The yarn should be wound around a chair back and secured loosely as shown (376). Wash the yarn as instructed on the yarn wrapper and leave to dry thoroughly before working again. A weight helps to remove the crinkles if anchored at the base of the hank.

376

When planning any crochet project involving hem lengths, it is worthwhile to work the crochet from top to hemline. By doing this, if a change in fashion indicates a shorter hemline, unpicking several rows is no problem.

Washing a finished garment

Washing finished garments after wearing should always take place before the yarn becomes too badly soiled. Always follow the instructions on the yarn wrapper and avoid over rubbing. Allow the garment to dry flat on a towel in a warm room or airing cupboard – never hang on a clothes line. Garments can be wrung out between two towels to remove excess water. Sometimes blocking and pressing improve the final appearance after washing.

Some finishing touches and trimmings

Fastenings

Many designs require some type of fastening to hold together two edges of fabric, eg the front edge of a coat or jacket. There are several possibilities: furrier's hooks and eyes for heavy crochet fabrics make a good and firm fastener. A length of crochet 1–2 cm wide and 20–30 cm long sewn on each side makes attractive ties. Buttons, either commercial or crochet moulds with appropriate sized buttonholes form a more conventional fastening. Whatever method you choose, it must form a part of the overall design of the outfit.

Buttons Button moulds can be covered with crochet, working in circles in a fine stitch (see Chapter 11).

377 and 378   A selection of crochet covered button moulds

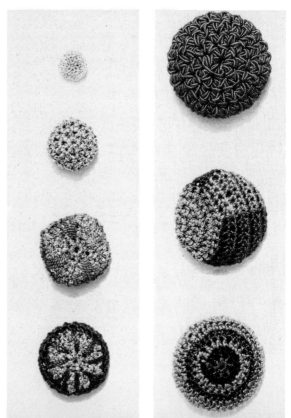

Buttonholes Buttonholes are usually made in a border edging of double crochet. Simply leave the required number of stitches unworked to give the size of the button diameter. Work the same number of chain stitches to correspond with the stitches missed and continue in the set crochet stitch. If the border is worked north to south, the buttonholes will be vertical. If, however, the border is worked as part of the main fabric and is worked east to west, the buttonholes will be horizontal. If a deeper stitch is being used, such as a treble or double treble stitch, a space will be left between the line of chain stitches and the missed stitches below. To reduce the space, work a single row of double crochet stitches round the opening, or work a buttonhole stitch using a needle and thread after the work is completed. For deeper stitches, it is usually found that the button will pass through the space between 2 stitches.

Mock rouleau loops can be used in crochet designs by working double crochet over a cord to give the desired thickness. The worked loops are placed along the crochet edge to form loops at regular intervals. The size of loop should just allow a ball button to pass through and should be sewn onto the other side of the garment.

379   Mock rouleau loops and buttons

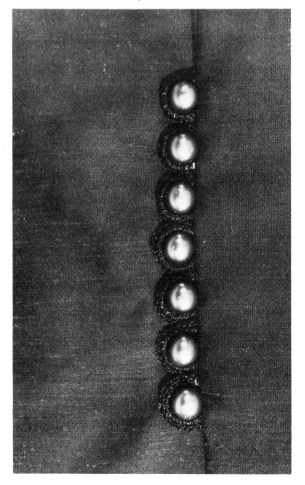

Belts and buckles

Crochet makes very suitable tie belts using the simple stitches. Strips of crochet can also be used with buckles and a decorative type of crochet buckle is shown here (380). Double crochet stitch is worked over a buckle shape using a lurex yarn and small wooden beads.

Waistbands (see pages 108 and 114)

381   Three methods of working the waistband for a skirt:

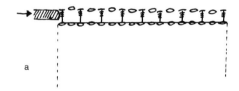

a

(a)   Elastic is threaded along the top edge which is worked with spaced triple trebles. 1 chain stitch forms the space. The elastic is cut to the required size and when the crochet edging is completed, the elastic is threaded over and under each triple treble stitch. Secure the ends very firmly. This method is ideal for outfits where the top over garment is placed outside the skirt. It makes a very neat, unbulky finish. The elastic can be dyed if the colour match is difficult.

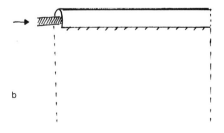

b

(b)   The top edge of the skirt can be turned over and hemmed very loosely down to enclose the elastic.

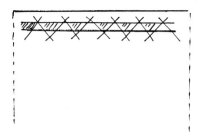

c

(c)   A casing is made for the elastic by working a line of herringbone stitches on the wrong side of the top edge of the skirt.

All these methods are only suitable for figure types where the hip measurement is larger than the waist by no more than 30 cm. For larger hip sizes, it would be better to have an opening on the side seam. This would require a zip fastener which should be sewn in neatly by hand.

Pockets

Pockets are useful additions to many designs for outer garments such as jackets and coats. Five types are given:

(a)   Pocket placed in a seamline
(b)   Patch
(c)   Flap
(d)   Bound or jetted pocket
(e)   Welt

(a)   *A pocket placed in a seamline*   The pocket shape is added to the seam on both sides of the sewing line. The shape takes the outline of the hand and should hang downwards. The outer line of the pocket is sewn together as a continuation of the main seamline. This is a very neat and inconspicuous pocket.

(b)   382   *Patch pocket*   The patch shape is applied to the fabric and surface crochet stitches used as a decorative technique to hold the pocket in place. The patch pocket can also be sewn into place using very neat and firm sewing stitches. In the sample, the crochet patch has been turned to add interest and a contrasting coloured yarn was used.

(c)   383   *Flap pocket*   The flap is lifted to find the pocket opening beneath. A pocket shape (known as the 'pocket bag' to form the inside) is placed on the inside. To make a flap pocket, work the main part of the garment leaving an opening the required size of pocket opening, ie miss the required number of stitches by working an equal number of chain stitches to cover the stitches missed. Continue to complete the main part of the crochet for the garment. The pocket bag inside is worked by placing crochet into the missed stitches, working 1 stitch into every missed stitch; double crochet is recommended. Continue to make a length twice the required pocket depth, plus the space left between the missed stitches and the line of chain stitches. This will vary according to the stitch being used for the main part of the garment. Fold crochet pocket bag in half and sew to the line of chain stitches. Sew up the sides of the pocket bag. The flap is worked by placing crochet along the top opening, that is the line of chain stitches with the pocket bag. Work crochet by placing the hook into each stitch along opening. The shape of the flap can be further outlined with a row of corded crochet. Allow the flap to lie downwards and press very lightly.

(d)   384   *Bound pocket*   A very neat pocket similar to a large buttonhole. Work the main part of the garment leaving a wide space of approximately 3 cm between the missed stitches and the line of chain stitches, that is the work has to be divided and the two sides worked separately to the correct depth before rejoining and working across the top of the pocket. The pocket bag is worked to shape and one open edge placed to each side of the pocket opening. Secure with pins to hold in place. Sew the sides of the pocket bag together. Work two pieces of crochet in double crochet, 3 cm deep and of the same width as the pocket opening. Fold in half and place folded edges to centre of pocket opening. Sew the open edges very neatly along the opening on the garment, securing the pocket bag at the same time. There will be four edges to be sewn down in one process – two from the bind, one from the garment and one from the pocket bag inside. Press lightly. The bind should always be worked with a fairly thin yarn if a double fabric is to be used. For thicker yarns the bind could be used in single thickness.

(e) 385 *Welt pocket* This type of pocket has a small strip called a welt, which is placed upwards with the pocket bag behind it inside the garment. Work as for a flap pocket but make the flap much smaller in depth. The welt is placed upwards and should be sewn down to the garment at each end.

Pockets can be a useful addition to any garment. They should always be very carefully planned and should form part of the overall look – their proportions should be correct, their position well chosen.

In the examples illustrated, different yarns have been used to emphasize the detail, but care should always be taken when using contrasting yarns for decoration.

All the pocket samples were worked on the horizontal line of the crochet fabric which is technically easiest to work. Diagonal pockets are quite possible, and a patch, can of course, be placed in any direction. For diagonal flap, welt and bound pockets more care and skill is needed for making the opening on the main garment, and uneven lines can result. If a diagonal line is imperative to your design, it might be best to work a seamline running along the line of the pocket, or to work your crochet in a north to south direction. A diagonal opening can be made by dividing the work and completing the crochet on either side of the pocket before rejoining the row again. Increasing and decreasing is required to give the diagonal line. The completion of the pocket would be the same as for horizontal designs.

18 – Irish Crochet

Crochet in Ireland usually brings to mind the crochet laces, which are the most outstanding type of crochet work seen in the country. Miss Honoria (Nano) Nagle is thought to have been responsible for introducing crochet to Ireland. She established the first Ursuline House as a school at Blackrock, Cork in 1771 and the South Presentation poor school in 1777, and it is known that crochet was taught by the nuns in these schools before 1847.[7] Miss Nano Nagle was educated in Paris during the year 1769 and it is believed she brought the art of crochet back to Ireland on her return there. Crochet was known on the continent in the sixteenth century.[8] During the period 1845–50 when there was much hardship due to famine and disease, the art of all hand work flourished in Ireland. Lace making was of great importance and a substantial source of income. Mr A S Cole quotes seven types of Irish lace made during this period:

1. Flat needle point lace
2. Raised needle point lace
3. Embroidery on net, either darning or chain stitch
4. Cut cambric or linen work in the style of guipure or appliqué lace
5. Drawn thread work in the style of Reticella and Italian cut points
6. Pillow lace in imitation of Devon lace
7. Crochet

It is the last type of lace which is to be discussed in this chapter. However, two comments should be made. First, that crochet lace is sometimes thought of as not being a 'true' lace, bobbin and needlemade laces being the only 'true' laces. Secondly, Irish crochet lace is also referred to as Irish point or point d'Irlande. The meaning of the word 'point' is uncertain – literally the word means a stitch – it is also used as an abbreviation for needlepoint laces such as gros point and rose point. Again, point is used with some bobbin made lace names.[9] Annette Feldman[10] says in her book that point means 'prick' which refers to the pricking of the parchment with the original design for the lace to be made.

Crochet in Ireland is mostly very fine work, using all the basic crochet techniques, and usually the double crochet stitch which resembles the buttonhole stitch of the needlemade laces – hence the collective term Irish Crochet Lace. During the period of the famine in Ireland of 1846, the production of crochet lace flourished in Cork and the surrounding areas. The Adelaide School under Mrs Meredith was well known. Further north in Clones, due to the efforts of Mrs Roberts and Mrs Hand, the crochet lace industry became very successful. Two variations emerged – the separate motif type with raised work featuring crochet in relief which was seen in the south, and the closed fine work of Clones. Crochet was successful because it was quicker to work than the other types of laces, using continuous lengths of yarn. Due to the changing social conditions of the time, both in Ireland and abroad, the success of Irish crochet lace fluctuated. However, it should be noted that during the period of 1880 to 1900 several organizations helped to promote the advancement of lace work, namely, the Irish Agricultural Organization Society, the Congested Districts Board and the Department of Agricultural and Technical Instruction. Financial help was given to both teachers and pupils. James Brennan, at one time head of the Cork and later the Dublin Art School and A S Cole, an art teacher, did much to improve the standard of design for lace working during this period. The Franco-German war of 1870 also increased the demand for Irish crochet lace because it meant a lack of continental laces in England.
386 A class in crochet lace in the late nineteenth century, organized by the Congested Districts Board. *Welch Collection, Ulster Museum*

Crochet laces were made in the schools, and much crochet was also worked indoors in the homes of families under very difficult conditions. If the weather permitted many families worked outside, including men, women and children, both boys and girls all doing their bit. Children would miss school in order to make money during the most difficult times. Many workers saved their earnings in order to buy a passage to America and much Irish crochet lace can be seen in that country today.

Cotton thread was used for the finest work, and was so fine that it was almost invisible. Linen was also used, and sometimes silk. Hooks were made from wire and placed into a piece of wood for the handle.

Crochet lace from Ireland was sold through 'patrons', 'agents' and 'businessmen' through exhibitions or individual contacts. Irish crochet lace, and its influence is seen in many countries including France, Italy, Sicily, Hungary (387), England and America during the last century. It is interesting to note here that Mlle Eleanore Riego de la Branchardiere,[11] a daughter of a Franco-Spanish nobleman who fled to England at the time of the French Revolution, visited the nuns of Blackrock convent in Dublin. She probably introduced an interest in fine crochet work to this country and wrote many books on crochet patterns between 1852 and 1854 which may be seen in the Victoria and Albert Museum Library. Fine crochet was unknown in England before 1820.

387 A blouse, c 1900, from an exhibition of Hungarian costume from Budapest shown at the Whitworth Art Gallery, Manchester, in 1979

Irish crochet lace was used for many articles, as well as trimming, edgings and insertions using the more simple lace designs. More intricate crochet could be seen in collars, cuffs, berthe collars, sleeves, blouses, boleros, bags (388) parasol covers, dress fronts, fichus, babies' bonnets, coats and short coaties. Some work was exceedingly fine and beautiful while some lacked good design and quality of workmanship. The quality of crochet lace was judged by its design, fineness of yarn and technical workmanship.

388   Nineteenth-century lace bag, probably Irish. *Crown copyright. Victoria and Albert Museum*

Irish crochet lace began to decline after its initial success during the famine period of 1845–50, but recovered its popularity again for a very prosperous period ending around 1910. Some reasons for the decline in the success of crochet lace both before and after the Edwardian period were:

1   The lack of strictness of perfect work by the workers. There was much freedom of work and it was

difficult to write down instructions. Pieces of crochet
were simply copied and worked by 'eye', and no two
people would make exactly the same motif.
2   The lack of artistic training and poor designs.
3   Inducements were made for cheap or inferior types
of crochet laces.
4   The production of very similar looking machine
made Irish crochet lace.

390   Lace blouses selling for 89s 6d and 55s 6d. From
the *Lady's Pictorial*, 2 May 1908. *Gawthorpe Hall.*

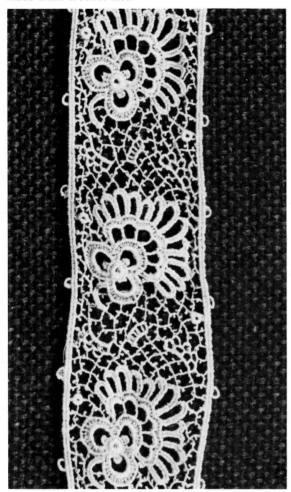

389   Machine-made Irish lace

It is interesting to note here that the first Irish Crochet
lace made by machine was worked in 1883[12] in
Switzerland and Germany. Machine embroidery in
cotton was worked onto a background of silk which
was then dissolved in chlorine or caustic soda, leaving
the machine embroidery of the Irish crochet. It was
also known as 'chemical', 'burnt' or 'Swiss lace'.

During the early part of this century patterns were
being produced in various publications covering the
individual motifs used in the heavier types of lace.
However, because of the very intricate designs,
explicit written explanations were difficult – patterns
were usually copied by one worker from another. The
motifs were placed onto a background of paper and
then tacked face downwards and joined together by
either a crochet stitch or a needlemade stitch.

391   Motifs tacked onto a background of brown
paper and some connecting crochet stitches applied.
Gawthorpe Hall.

For good results, a full outline of the article to be
made, the design of each motif and the placing of each
motif within the outline should be prepared. Often an
edging line of crochet would be worked round the
outer edge. Instructions were given in *Fancy Needlework Illustrated, Needlecraft* and various books
edited by Flora Klickman. Many of these publications
are available in the Victoria and Albert Library in
London. Today, various crochet patterns appear from
time to time with the influence of the Irish raised rose
very evident. Crochet lace is still available in Ireland
and figure 392 shows a dress trimmed with lace.

392 Hand crochet over pink silk. *The Mary O'Donnell Boutique, Dublin.*
There is still a demand for crochet of good design used for wearable garments.

The following types of crochet lace in Ireland were quoted by Mr Ben Lindsey, a Dublin lace dealer, in his account of Irish Lace published in 1886–8:

Plain and lace crochet – Cork
Greek crochet – Clones
Venetian crochet – Clones
Spanish crochet – Clones
Jesuit crochet – Clones
Imitation guipure, knotted and lifted guipure – Clones.

Plain and lace crochet – Cork   The plain crochet lace is slightly coarser and more regular in design than Venetian style laces. The crochet is made in one piece and it is the simplest and most elementary form. Edgings, d'oileys, articles for toilet use and antimacassars were made using the plain crochet trimmings. Lace crochet features separate motifs joined together with crochet chain stitches or needle point lace stitches to form a joining background.

Greek crochet   Rather similar to reticella work with lines of double crochet bars. The bars have little picots and the work looks very much like the needlemade buttonhole lace known as reticella work. A very fine tambour hook and equally fine thread were used to produce some very good quality pieces.

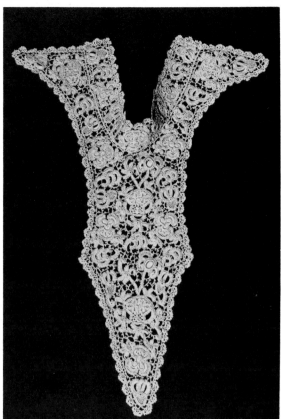

394   Venetian gros point – crochet, c 1900. *Crown copyright. Victoria and Albert Museum*

Venetian crochet   The various types of Venetian needlemade laces were copied using the double crochet stitch to form some beautiful pieces of work. There were several different varieties made which followed the style of the Venetian gros point with heavier designs and large areas worked in relief, and Venetian rose point with flowers and smaller motifs with some padded and knobbly caterpillar lines of raised work. This lace is distinguished by its richness of detail. Some people say that 'rose' is a corruption of 'raised'. Point de neige was another type of Venetian needlemade lace imitated with smaller flowers and fewer raised areas in double crochet stitches. Tiny picots gave it a snow flake appearance. Sometimes these Venetian crochet laces are referred to as point de Venise and point d'Irlande, and were used by leaders of fashion in Paris, New York, Vienna and Brussels. Figure 424 shows a dress by Paquin dated 1902.

Spanish crochet   It is thought that specimens of lace from Spain reached Ireland after the monasteries were dissolved in 1830. Some designs were based on these pieces. Spain, where there was a great love of lace, may have imported some pieces and also many fine needlemade examples were made there. Again the Venetian needlemade lace influence can be seen. The lace consisted of leaf shapes with raised centres and the joining crochet is rather irregular with picots.

393   Venetian gros point, 1878, needlemade. *National Museum of Ireland*

Scalloped edgings would also feature on this lace.

Jesuit crochet   This lace took its name from the tradition that a Jesuit procured the first Venetian lace patterns used in Ireland.[13] Specimens from which copies were made had belonged to this religious order. Lace of this type was more intricate than the Spanish examples and the motifs were larger with some raised areas and some 'brides' with triple picots featured in the joining lines.

Imitation guipure, knotted and lifted guipure – Clones   Lace of this type is much finer and consists chiefly of brides worked close and tight. There are some small objects of design and the whole effect is plain and simple. There is great excellence in the work due to the fineness of threads. The knotted guipures developed from a Venetian model and together with the lifted guipures have a light and very elegant appearance. Most have scalloped edgings and feature picots. Lace of this type is not always appreciated: it was difficult to work, more expensive and comparatively rare.

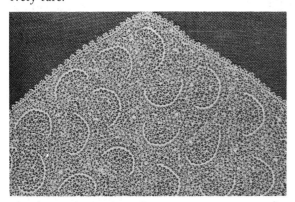

395   Part of a berthe collar, c 1900. Tiny circles of double crochet appear on the surface. *Crown copyright. Victoria and Albert Museum*

It will be seen from this brief outline of the various crochet laces made in Ireland that there is a very wide variety. Many examples were made as copies of lace made by other techniques, such as the needlemade types, and came from different countries. With the process of improvement or the progress of decay the work has undergone changes in style and design, which in some cases leaves no trace of the original. Some ideas and designs for crochet motifs are given in the following pages together with some techniques employed in the raised type of Irish crochet lace. Double crochet is the basic stitch for the main designs with chain stitches forming the joining lines in the majority of work. The chain stitch can be further decorated with different types of picots.

Using the Irish crochet lace as a starting point, try designing your own ideas. Draw your own motifs and place the outline onto the shape for a complete article. The lace should be seen as a whole and complete design. Each motif should be designed within its own outline and the crochet stitches selected. After trying some of the instructions given here, it is hoped that individual ideas will emerge from your original draw-

ings by experimenting with different yarns. These motifs can then be joined together using the traditional techniques, or the motifs can be arranged and sewn onto a background fabric as shown in the pale blue outfit in colour plate 5, between pages 92/3 and the parasol cover in figure 396, opposite.

Six methods are given for joining the motifs to form a fabric:

1   Needlemade techniques.
2   Plain undecorated chain stitches.
3   Chain stitches covered with double crochet.
4   Chain stitches decorated with picots – there are various different kinds.
5   Chain stitches decorated with the Clones knot.
6   Motifs sewn directly onto a net background – this may be either a commercially made net or a crochet net.

For all the examples above, an additional crochet edging can be worked when the motifs are all joined together.

For the joining techniques 1 to 5 the motifs are placed face downwards onto a firm base (391). For method 1 the needlemade stitches used for joining are found in the books listed in the bibliography. When all the needlemade stitches are worked and the motifs secured together, the lace may be removed from the foundation base.

397   An insertion 7.5 cm wide, completely reversible. Twisted threads form the filling stitches and these are decorated with picots. *Crown copyright. Victoria and Albert Museum*

For joining techniques 2 to 5 plain chain stitches with or without the named additions are used to hold the motifs together, working to and fro from one motif to another, slip stitching along the work to place the chains in a connecting position. Several different picots are explained, all of which may be added to the chained joining stitches. The symbol used for a picot is shown on page 134 and any of the following methods can be used for this symbol. Various examples of joining chains with the picot symbol are given in this chapter and may be used to work between the motifs as a joining mesh, or used to make a complete background fabric for the motifs to be sewn onto later.

The various types of picots

1   *Plain upright picots*   Work 6 chain. 1 double crochet into the 6th chain from the hook. 1 picot made.

A smaller picot can be made by placing fewer chain stitches into the loop and working 1 slip stitch in place of a double crochet.

2 *Drooping picot* Work 6 chain, remove hook, insert hook into the 5th chain from hook, replace working stitch and draw through chain. Again various sizes can be worked depending on the number of chain stitches in the loop.

3 *Double picots* Onto a chain length work 5 chain, 1 double crochet into the 5th chain from hook, turn loop from right to left and work 4 chain and 1 double crochet into loop.

4 *Multiple picots* Onto a chain length, work *5 chain stitches, 1 slip stitch into the 5th stitch from hook*, repeat from * to * once for each loop of picot required. Work 1 slip stitch into the chain stitch before first loop to hold all picot loops together – 3 loops form a good shape.

5 *The Clones knot* This knot stitch can be worked in place of a picot. Also known as Post stitch.

398 *Left* Groups of 4 knots worked onto the chain filling stitches.

399–402 Making the Clones knot.

401 Place yarn over hook and draw yarn through the chain stitch and through all the loops on the hook.

402 Work 1 double crochet into stitch at base of knot.

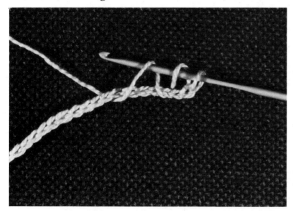

399 Yarn being placed around the chain length. Repeat until approximately 20 loops lie on the hook.

400 Insert hook into chain stitch nearest the hook still uncovered.

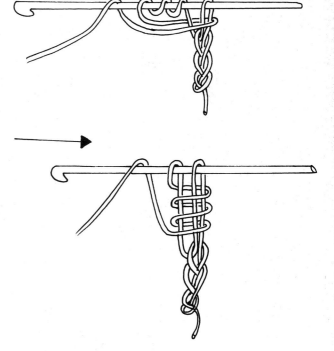

403 and 404 Modifications of the Clones knot which can be used with the chain stitch. Both methods form a knotted type of chain stitch.

6   *Chained background or commercial net used for crochet motifs*   In place of the temporary foundation used in the first five examples, a complete chained background, using picots if wished, is made to form the background for the motifs. The background is made to the required shape and the motifs applied. Careful placing is essential. Alternatively, a commercial net may be used as the foundation and the motifs are then sewn onto this background. Figure 396 uses a commercial net which is further backed with satin for each section of the parasol.

405   A collar made up of large motifs joined together with three different background stitches.
  (i)   Double crochet bars and chain picots.
  (ii)   Chain stitch bars and chain stitch picots.
  (iii) Chain stitch bars with Clones knot.

406–11   Six crochet patterns which can be used for joining motifs or as a complete background.
The illustrations show a basic foundation of chain stitch, but all the backgrounds can be worked directly onto an existing crochet edge of the motifs to be joined. Some adjustment of stitches and length of chains would be necessary.
406   Basic chained background with 1 double crochet stitch placed in the centre loop of each length of chain
407   A small 3-chain loop (could be called a picot) is placed between the 2 joining double crochet stitches
408   Similar to 406 but 2 picots worked on each loop.
409   Similar to 406 but a triple picot worked on the centre of the loop. On the following row the 2 joining double crochet stitches are placed between and behind the picots
410   Double treble stitch worked between lengths of chain stitches.
411   A more complicated background, usually worked by attaching the chain stitches onto motifs already tacked onto a background base. On the first row, work 1 slip stitch into the 20th chain from hook, turn work and work 4 double crochet up the chains just made, turn work, *8 chain, slip stitch into the 7th chain on the foundation from last slip stitch, turn work. Work 4 double crochet up the chains just made*, repeat from * to * to end. See arrows marked 1–14. At the end of the row, continue working in double crochet over the un-worked chain stitches of each loop. See arrows marked 15–18. Continue following the symbols in the direction of the arrows.

   All the designs illustrated can be modified by working different numbers of chain stitches and altering the type and size of picots used.

   The other feature seen in Irish crochet laces is the raised design lines worked in double crochet. These lines can form part of the motif or may be used as additions.

Key for figs 406–411

← Indicates the starting position and direction of work. When more than one arrow appears, work from one arrow to the next in numerical order

O   Chain

+   Double crochet

⬭   Picot – select the picot of your choice

‡   Double treble

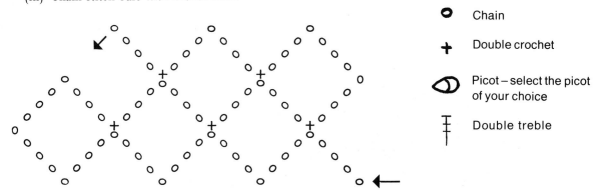

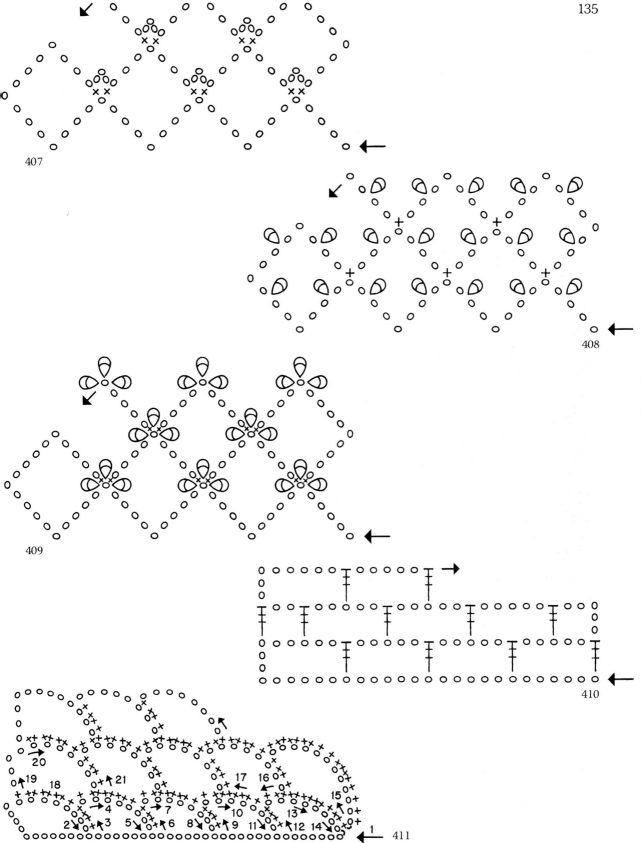

407

408

409

410

411

Figure 398 shows the raised lines of double crochet worked over thicker yarns to throw parts of the design into high relief. The method of working over the yarn is shown in figure 412 – a continuous length, and figure 413 – a circle. Lengths and circles worked in this manner may be used without further crochet stitches being added or as the centre of larger pieces being surrounded by crochet stitches either working over several pieces of yarn again, or without any further padding. Great care is required when working double crochet over padding yarns; the threads should lie parallel and not be crossed, the tension of the padding yarns should be correct – not too slack and not too taut. The double crochet stitches worked over the padding yarns should be correctly and evenly spaced with no gaps. Sometimes other stitches are worked over the padding yarns, such as treble stitches. Raised crochet, working double crochet over several pieces of yarn may be used to round off and make firm the edges of shapes made without padding yarns.

414   Petals of the flower motifs using this technique which illustrate motifs 4, 6 and 8 below.

415   A selection of some motifs which may be worked in crochet using cords in several examples. Written instructions are given as a guide but it is difficult to give very detailed explanations, and it is advisable to look at the photographs illustrating the actual work. The motifs were used on the parasol cover (396) and the blouson top (colour plate 5 between pages 92/3).

412 and 413

Most of the crochet worked in this manner requires washing and starching before use. Recommended yarn for these motifs is the Coats mercer crochet yarn which is available in various thicknesses, mostly in white. Colours are available in the thicker yarns.

417   Crochet worked to illustrate motifs 7 and 9
418   Crochet worked to illustrate motifs 1 and 3

416   A small bag illustrating the use of a moderately fine yarn with a small motif and crochet edgings. This would make a suitable starting point if you are not familiar with the very fine yarns. The bag is made in a No. 10 Coats mercer crochet yarn with a No. 1.25 ISR crochet hook.

Colour plate 7, between pages 92/3, illustrates a modified use of the Irish crochet technique involving padded circles. Various Twilley yarns are used in shades of orange and red. Each motif is made separately, placed onto a pattern outline and sewn together on the wrong side.

Instructions for motif 1

Two variations are given. No. 50 Coats mercer crochet yarn and a No. 0.75 ISR crochet hook.
Wrap the yarn round a pencil or a No. 7.00 ISR crochet hook, 26 times. Remove yarn from pencil and work 21 double crochet into the centre (see figure 413). Slip stitch into first double crochet worked.
Round 2   1 chain to count as 1 double crochet, (1 half treble, 1 treble, 1 half treble) into next double crochet, 1 double crochet into next double crochet. *1 double crochet into next double crochet, (1 half treble, 1 treble, 1 half treble) into next double crochet, 1 double crochet into next double crochet*, repeat from * to * 6 times. Slip stitch to chain stitch at start of round.

Alternative motif

Use same yarn and hook. Wrap the yarn round a pencil 26 times. Remove yarn from pencil and work 24 double crochet into the centre. Slip stitch into first double crochet worked.

Round 2   *6 chain, miss 2 double crochet, 1 double crochet into next double crochet,* repeat from * to * 8 times. See figure 418.

Instructions for motif 2

No. 50 Coats mercer crochet yarn and a No. 0.75 ISR crochet hook.

Wind the yarn round a pencil at least 24–30 times.

Round 1   Remove yarn from pencil and work 20 double crochet over the cords. Slip stitch into the first double crochet worked.

Round 2   *10 chain, miss 1 double crochet, slip stitch into next double crochet*, repeat from * to * 9 times. There will be 9 loops in total – work 7 chain, slip stitch into the 3rd chain up of the first loop of this round.

Round 3   3 chain to count as 1 treble. 7 treble into first loop. *8 treble into same loop but at the same time catching the next chain loop (the trebles will be worked downwards towards the centre of the motif). Slip stitch into 8th treble from hook forming a pleat. 8 trebles into same 10 chain loop,* repeat from * to * to complete round. 8 trebles down remaining loop, slip stitch into 8th stitch from hook. 1 slip stitch into the 3rd chain at start of this round.

Figure 396 shows the use of this motif.

Instructions for motif 3

No. 40 Coats mercer crochet yarn and a No. 0.75 ISR crochet hook.

Centre piece   Wind a thick yarn such as Twilley's *Knitcot, Health* vest cotton or *Stalite* round a No. 10 crochet hook 10 times. Remove yarn and using the Coats No. 40 yarn work 50 double crochet into the centre. Cut the ends of the thick yarn to trim. Leave Coats yarn on motif and place stitch onto a safety pin.

The surrounding outer strip   Take a new ball of Coats No. 40 yarn and work 40 double crochet over 3 lengths of thick yarn approximately 35 cm long, leaving a 4 cm length free at the start. Secure stitch and cut the Coats yarn but do not cut the thick yarns.

Place the surrounding strip just made above the centre motif with the 4 cm free end and the 40 double crochet placed to the right-hand side hanging freely. Work from the Coats yarn used for the centre motif, work over the 3 thicknesses of thick yarn, work 1 double crochet into next 25 double crochet of centre motif. Place the 4 cm free end of strip with double crochet to form the outer loop standing away from the centre motif so that the chained edge of the double crochet is towards the centre; work 1 double crochet stitch placing hook over the 3 thicknesses of thick yarn and over and between the double crochet on strip. Work 40 double crochet.

Adjust the thick yarns to form a good shape and continue working over the 3 thicknesses of yarn. *Work 1 double crochet into next 6 double crochet, 1 picot (5-chain type as shown in Chapter 5), 1 double

crochet into same stitch as last double crochet worked,* 3 times, 1 double crochet in next 6 double crochet. Leave thick yarns hanging free. 1 double crochet into next stitch, 1 slip stitch into next stitch. *5 chain, miss 2 stitches, 1 double crochet into next stitch*, 14 times. Secure stitch and secure all thick yarns before cutting. The joining lines placed between the outer strip and the centre motif: work from the wrong side with surrounding strip on top. Join in Coats yarn to centre motif on lower right-hand side. Work 1 double crochet into next 2 stitches, 1 double crochet into stitch on opposite side of surrounding loop. Miss 1 stitch on centre motif, 1 double crochet into next 3 stitches. 1 treble into opposite stitch on surrounding loop. Miss 1 stitch on centre motif, 1 double crochet into next 3 stitches. 1 quadruple treble in the diagonally opposite stitch on surrounding loop. Miss 1 stitch on centre motif, 1 double crochet in next 3 stitches. 1 quadruple treble in the diagonally opposite stitch on surrounding loop. Miss 1 stitch on centre motif, 1 double crochet into next 2 stitches. 1 treble in opposite stitch on surrounding loop. Miss 1 stitch on centre motif, 1 double crochet into next 2 stitches. 1 double crochet in opposite stitch on surrounding loop. Slip stitch into remaining stitches and fasten off all ends.

This motif can be modified and adapted to form various different patterns. See figure 418.

Instructions for motif 4

No. 40 Coats mercer crochet yarn and a No. 0.75 ISR crochet hook.

Cut a length of thick yarn 17 cm long. Work double crochet stitches over this yarn with the Coats No. 40 thread leaving 0.5 cm unworked each end. The double crochet stitches should not be overcrowded.

When the yarn is covered turn work and add a second length of thick yarn, taking it from the supply ball. Work in double crochet over both thick yarns, working 1 double crochet into each single double crochet of previous row. Leave 5 cm with single row of double crochet – approximately 30 double crochet – and loop back to form the first outer loop or petal. Slip stitch to hold in place.

Place the start of crochet length behind work and slip stitch into the first double crochet made to form cone shape of foundation. Adjust the cord to make a good shape.

Work over single thickness of thick yarn, work 2 double crochet, slip stitch into opposite double crochet of previous petal, 2 double crochet, slip stitch into opposite double crochet of previous petal, 26 double crochet, 1 double crochet into double crochet of centre foundation, 1 cm from base of last petal, repeat from * to * making 11 petals. Adjust the thick yarn to make a good petal shape between each double crochet placed onto the centre foundation. Fasten off all threads on the wrong side and cut ends.

The centre motif   Slip stitch to the inside of the cone foundation to one side of end point. 6 chain to form first bar to centre circle. 1 quadruple treble into inside of cone foundation on the opposite side of point. *1 chain, miss 10 double crochet after last bar stitch made, 1 double treble in next double crochet,* 3 times. 1 chain, slip stitch into 5th chain at start of centre to form a small circle. From the right side of motif work, *2 double crochet into centre circle, slip stitch behind next bar,* 5 times. Fasten off yarn and darn in all ends to neaten. See figure 414.

Instructions for motif 5

No. 60 Coats mercer crochet yarn and a No. 0.75 ISR crochet hook.

This is a more intricate motif to make and it is difficult to make two flowers exactly the same.

Round 1 Wind the Coats yarn round a pencil 24 times. Slip the yarn off the pencil and work 24 double crochet into the circle. Slip stitch to join to first double crochet made.

Round 2 1 chain to count as 1 double crochet. 1 double crochet into each double crochet to end of round. Slip stitch into the first chain.

Round 3 3 chain to count as 1 treble. *1 chain, 1 treble into next double crochet*, repeat from * to * to end of round. 1 chain, slip stitch into 3rd chain at start of round. There should be 24 trebles with a space between each treble.

Round 4 Slip stitch into first 1-chain space, 1 chain to count as 1 double crochet. *4 chain, miss one 1-chain space, 1 double crochet into next 1-chain space,* repeat from * to * until 11 chain loops have been made. 4 chain, slip stitch into first chain at start of round. 12 loops in total.

Round 5 Into each 4-chain loop work: (1 double crochet, 3 treble, 1 double crochet), slip stitch into first double crochet worked.

Round 6 1 chain. Slip stitch into first free 1-chain space working behind petals of last round. 1 chain to count as 1 double crochet. *5 chain, 1 double crochet into next free 1-chain space,* repeat from * to * until 11 chain loops have been made. 5 chain, slip stitch into first chain at start of round. All loops should lie behind petals of previous round.

Round 7 Into each 5-chain loop work: (1 double crochet, 4 treble, 1 double crochet), slip stitch into first double crochet worked.

Round 8 5 chain, slip stitch into space between the first and second petal of previous round, place chain behind petal working into the bar at the back of petal. Work 6 more chain lengths slip stitching between petals. There should be 7 loops in total.

The outer long petals Turn work. *16 chain. 1 double crochet into the 6th chain from hook, (2 chain, miss 2 chain, 1 double crochet into next chain) 3 times. 1 chain, slip stitch into first 5-chain loop. Turn work. (2 chain, miss 1 double crochet, 1 double crochet into next 2-chain space) 4 times. 2 chain. 1 double crochet into last space. Turn work.
1 chain, 1 double crochet into first space. (2 chain, 1 double crochet into next 2-chain space) 4 times. 1 chain. Slip stitch into the 5-chain loop. Turn work. (2 chain, miss 1 double crochet, 1 double crochet into next 2-chain space) 4 times. 2 chain. 1 double crochet into last space. Turn work.

1 chain, 1 double crochet into first space. (2 chain, 1 double crochet into next 2-chain space) 4 times. 1 chain. Slip stitch into the 5-chain loop.* Slip stitch into the next 5-chain loop and work 6 more petals repeating * to * for each petal.

Turn work and complete the surrounding cording: Take a single piece of thick cotton yarn for the cording and work all further double crochet over this cord. Leave an end of cord approximately 8 cm long hanging free, and place cord behind each stitch to be worked. Work approximately 3 double crochet into each space all round the first long petal. When the first petal is complete, work 6 double crochet up the next petal and slip stitch into opposite stitch on first petal. Complete the other petals in the same manner.

The stem Continue to work over the cord, take in the cord from the starting point leaving a space approximately 1 cm of unworked yarn. Work 10 double crochet over both sets of cord to hold in place. Work 40 double crochet over single cord. Turn work and place 1 double crochet over cord and over the first length of cord just worked with double crochet for 50 stitches. Work 15 double crochet over double cord to complete the stem to first petal. Cut thick cord free. Turn work and place 1 double crochet without cord into each double crochet of stem working round full length to the other side of the flower. Break off yarn and darn in ends. See figure 396.

Instructions for motif 6

No. 40 Coats mercer crochet yarn and a No. 0.75 ISR crochet hook.

Wind a thick yarn 10 times round a large pencil or a No. 10 crochet hook. Remove yarn and with Coats No. 40 work 40 double crochet into the centre. Slip stitch to the first double crochet made. Continue to work over a single thickness of the thick yarn, work 1 chain to count as 1 double crochet, work 1 double crochet into each double crochet of first round. Slip stitch to first double crochet of round.

Final round *Continue to work over single thickness of thick yarn, work 20 double crochet. Miss 4 double crochet on last round, one slip stitch into next double crochet,* repeat from * to * 8 times. Break off yarns and darn in ends. See figure 414.

Instructions for motif 7

No. 60 Coats mercer crochet yarn and a No. 0.6 ISR crochet hook.

Round 1 Wind a thick yarn round pencil 4 times or place working yarn round pencil 40 times to make centre shape. Remove yarn from pencil and work 30 double crochet into the centre. Slip stitch to first double crochet made.

Round 2 Work over single thickness of thick yarn for *all* the following instructions:
(1 double crochet, 12 treble, 1 double crochet, miss 5 stitches on ring, 1 double crochet into next stitch) 5 times. Slip stitch into first double crochet of this round.

Round 3 Work as last round working (1 double crochet, 15 treble, 1 double crochet) for each petal and slip stitch to double crochet between each petal of second round.

Round 4   Work as last round working (1 double crochet, 18 treble, 1 double crochet) for each petal and slip stitch to double crochet between each petal of last round.

Round 5   Work as last round working (1 double crochet, 21 treble, 1 double crochet) for each petal and slip stitch to double crochet between each petal of last round.

Round 6   Work as last round working (1 double crochet, 25 treble, 1 double crochet) for each petal and slip stitch to double crochet between each petal of last round.

Break off yarn and darn in all ends.
See figure 417.

Instructions for motif 8

No. 40 Coats mercer crochet yarn and a No. 1.00 ISR crochet hook.
Wind a thick yarn round a No. 12 ISR crochet hook 14 times. Do not cut the yarns but remove from large hook.

Round 1   With Coats yarn work 58 double crochet into centre working over thick yarn. Slip stitch to first double crochet of round.

Round 2   Working over the thick yarn, work (1 double crochet into next 8 double crochet, 2 double crochet into next double crochet) 6 times. 1 double crochet into last 4 stitches. This completes the foundation centre.

The petals   20 chain. 1 treble into 7th chain from hook. (1 chain, miss 1 chain, 1 treble into next chain) 3 times. (1 chain, miss 1 chain, 1 double crochet into next chain) 3 times. 1 chain. Slip stitch into next double crochet on foundation centre. 1 chain, miss 1 double crochet on foundation centre. Slip stitch into next double crochet on foundation centre. Turn work. (1 chain, 1 double crochet into next double crochet) 3 times. (1 chain, 1 treble into next treble) 5 times. Turn work. 5 chain to count as 1 treble and 1 chain for space, miss 1 treble and one 1-chain space, (1 treble into next treble, 1 chain) 4 times. (1 double crochet into next double crochet, 1 chain) 3 times. Slip stitch into next 5 double crochet on foundation centre. This completes 1 petal. Repeat these instructions to form 7 more petals.

To work the cording round each petal: work over a single thickness of thick cotton yarn for all double crochet stitches. Join yarn into base of 1 petal and work 3 double crochet stitches into each space. At the top of each petal work 7 double crochet into each corner space. Work 1 double crochet into the foundation centre between the base of each petal. When all the cording is complete, break off both yarns and secure ends.

Final round   With right side of flower facing, join yarn to top left-hand corner of petal at base of space, *work 7 chain, slip stitch into corresponding position on next petal, 7 chain and slip stitch to original position – this forms the line for double crochet, joining two petals. Work (3 double crochet, 1 picot, 3 double

crochet, 1 picot, 3 double crochet) over double chain length. Work 1 double crochet into next 3 double crochet, 1 picot, 1 double crochet into next 4 double crochet, 1 picot, 1 double crochet into next 4 double crochet, 1 picot, 1 double crochet into next 3 double crochet,* repeat from * to * to complete the flower. Break off yarn and secure the ends. See figure 414.

Instructions for motif 9

No. 40 Coats mercer crochet yarn and a No. 1.00 ISR crochet hook.

Work *all* crochet stitches over a thick cotton yarn. Begin by working approximately 20 double crochet leaving a length of yarn 4 cm long.

The coil   work 24 double crochet approximately, twist coil to lie over yarn with double crochet stitches just worked and make 1 slip stitch into the 25th double crochet from hook. This forms a loop. Work 5 double crochet and work next coil of 24 double crochet. The number of stitches worked, can of course, be varied to suit the requirements of the design.

In figure 414 the eight petal flower has a length of coiled loops placed round a double crochet padded circle in the centre.

Lace edging used on parasol (396)

No. 40 Coats mercer crochet yarn and a No. 0.75 ISR crochet hook.
Tension: 11 chain = 2.5 cm.
One picot = 5 chain, slip stitch into 5th chain from hook.
Make a chain length multiple of 12 + 1.

Row 1   1 chain to count as 1 double crochet. 1 double crochet into 3rd chain from hook. 1 double crochet into each stitch to end. Turn work.

Row 2   3 chain to count as 1 double crochet and one 1-chain space. 1 double crochet into 6th stitch from hook. *1 chain, miss 1 double crochet, 1 double crochet into next double crochet*, repeat from * to * to end of row. Turn work.

Row 3   1 chain to count as 1 double crochet. 1 double crochet into first one 1-chain space. *1 double crochet into next double crochet, 1 double crochet into next 1-chain space,* repeat from * to * to end of row. 1 double crochet into last stitch. Turn work.

Row 4   1 chain to count as 1 double crochet. 1 double crochet into 3rd stitch from hook. *5 chain, miss 3 double crochet, 1 double crochet into next 3 double crochet,* repeat from * to * to end, ending with 1 double crochet into last 2 double crochet instead of 3. Turn work.

Row 5   1 chain to count as 1 double crochet. 8 double crochet into 5-chain loop. *1 double crochet into next 3 double crochet. 9 double crochet into 5-chain loop,* repeat from * to * to last two stitches. 1 double crochet into each stitch. Turn work.

Row 6   9 chain, miss 11 double crochet. 1 double

Right
419–422   Further suggestions for using the motifs

crochet into next double crochet. *8 chain, miss 11 double crochet, 1 double crochet into next double crochet,* repeat from * to * to end of row. Turn work.
Row 7   1 chain to count as 1 double crochet, 2 double crochet into next 8-chain loop. 1 picot, (3 double crochet into same loop, 1 picot) twice, 3 double crochet into same loop. 1 slip stitch into middle double crochet between loops,* (3 double crochet into next loop, 1 picot) 3 times. 3 double crochet into same loop. 1 slip stitch into the middle double crochet between loops,* repeat from * to * to end of row. Break off yarn and darn in ends.

423   Youghal crochet dress, about 1906–8 *National Museum of Ireland.*

424   Design for a mousseline dress with a broad hem by the Paris designer Paquin, 1898–1909. *Victoria and Albert Museum*

Further reading

I would like to mention the following books which cover in various forms some aspect of crochet work in Ireland:

Elizabeth Boyle, *The Irish Flowerers**
S F A Caulfeild, *Encyclopedia of Victorian Needlework*
A S Cole, *A Renascence of the Irish Art of Lace Making* London 1888†. (17510 e 7). (Mr Cole was an art teacher)
Pat Earnshaw, *The Identification of Lace*
Annette Feldman, *Handmade Lace and Patterns*
Sylvia Groves, *The History of Needlework Tools and Accessories*
Ben Lindsey, *Irish Lace – its origin and history,* Dublin 1886† (17510 d 1) (Ben Lindsey was a Dublin lace dealer).

Ada K Longfield, *The Guide to the Collection of Lace**
Mrs Meredith, *The Lacemakers*, London 1865†. (250 n
236) (Mrs Meredith was a proprietor of a famine lace
school in Cork).
Mrs Palliser, *A History of Lace*, London, 1910
Patricia Wardle, *Victorian Lace*.

Specimens of Irish crochet lace may be seen in:
  The Victoria and Albert Museum in London
  The Woodstock Museum, Oxfordshire
  Gawthorpe Hall, Lancashire‡
  The Costume Museum, Bath
  The Ulster Folk and Transport Museum, Cultra
  Manor, Holywood, Co. Down.
  The National Museum of Ireland, Kildare Street,
  Dublin 2

* At the time of writing available from the Ulster Folk Museum.
† Bodleian Library, Oxford. Shelf reference numbers given in
brackets.
‡ Gawthorpe Hall is part of the Rachel Kay-Shuttleworth Trust.
Items from this collection are available for private study from
Mondays to Fridays only during the academic year. Written
application should be made well in advance to the Curator,
Gawthorpe Hall, Padiham, Burnley, Lancs, BB12 8UA Tel:
0282–72177.

19 – Turkish crochet

Textiles and needlework in their widest sense have been traditional amongst the Turkish people for a very long time. Embroidery and lace making form a major contribution. Decorative embroidery is still practised today both in the home and in schools such as the Olgunlaşhma Institutes in Istanbul, Izmir, Ankara and Trabzon, and crochet is an important element of this work.

Most crochet designs were handed down from mother to daughter, and between friends, with no written instructions. The same practice still exists today. Many old examples of crochet may be seen in museums in Turkey and in private collections. Crochet work in Turkey is seen in the making of laces, bags, cushion covers, caps worn by men while praying and as a trimming for many household articles. Traditional woollen knitted socks also show a crochet braiding used as part of the design around the top edge. Most examples were made during the last century.

First the Turkish laces. There are two areas where laces are used – lace for household articles in the home, and lace for personal articles. Lace in the home is used as a trimming on many articles such as bed linen, hand towels, table napkins, table mats, covers for chair back and arm pieces. Lace for bed linen is usually white, made of cotton or linen, using a thread similar to Coats No. 80 mercer crochet yarn. The crochet lace is worked as an edging or as an insertion. Some edgings used for the bed linen have names, for example, 'Mother-in-law's tongue' depicts the shape of an iris leaf in the design, and the 'Bride's fan' illustrates a fan shape made of long trebles radiating outwards in three rows. They are very beautiful and the technique excellent.

Today, crochet is used for such items in the house as table mats and glass mats, articles in the bedroom, covers for water jugs, saucepan holders, holders for guest towels and divan covers. However, the lace today is more often made from man-made fibres which have been chemically dyed and the crochet is not as fine as in earlier work.

425 Part of a white lace edging used on sheets

illustrating the *ilik* shape. This refers to the little circular motifs like a buttonhole – the edging is 8 cm deep at its widest reducing to 5 cm. The repeat pattern measures 8 cm. *Property of Mügül Andrews*

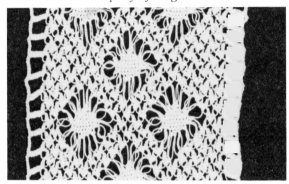

426 Part of a white lace insertion – both edges being attached to the fabric – suitable for bed linen. The lace measures 8 cm and illustrates the Solomon's knot stitch, some stitches being very elongated around the centre motifs which are closely worked in double crochet stitch. *Property of Mügül Andrews.*

Personal lace consists largely of the very fine narrow laces used for trimmings, either as a braid or a more decorative edging. The lace is seen as a decoration on such articles as sashes (*kusaklar*), scarves (*cevreler*), large handkerchieves (*mendiller*), towels (*havlular*), head squares (*yemeniler*), squares used for covering and wrapping personal clothes (*bohçalar*). The young girls prepare their dowry by making lace for these articles, and it is known by the name *oya*. For example, each girl may prepare as many as 25 head squares displaying very beautiful and different oyas (*oyalar*). The best quality lace and the most highly valued would be extremely fine, and only the finest thread would be used, either cotton, linen or silk. Sometimes very tiny beads would be incorporated. The very best technique used for making oyas is the needlemade technique and only the more able needlewoman could produce the best quality oya. A needlemade oya can be worked directly onto the fabric inserting the sewing needle into the hemmed edge of the square. The oya made solely with a needle is called *iğne oyasi*. An example of the *iğne oyasi* is shown in colour plate 6 between pages 92/3. The stitch is a type of buttonhole loop stitch, but uses a double knot to each loop made, making a very firm and tight loop – quite different from any other type of needlemade lace.

427 Examples of *Tiğ oyasi* all made with a crochet hook. Given to the author by Professor Kenan Özbel.

The oyas are very colourful and the designs take the form of flowers, fruit and leaves. Some are direct replicas in miniature of Turkish wild flowers such as

a)

b)

c)

violets, orchids, pansies, roses, jasmins, carnations, strawberries, blackberries, mulberries and peppers. Many carry a message.

The oya used on the headscarves were used as a type of expression and form part of the ethnic culture of the population in Anatolia. Because of their way of life and tradition, a young woman did not speak freely to her mother-in-law until her first baby was born or until two years had passed. She would use the 'language of the oya' as a form of communication – using for example – the red rose and carnation for happiness and love. Red peppers for her 'cross moods'; a dentilated shaped edging in the form of tomb stones indicated her feelings toward her mother-in-law – the colour denoting the nature of these feelings.

The dowry would be seen by her friends and relatives thus showing off her handiwork and favourite patterns and designs. These designs were copied and modified which led to certain patterns being found in particular regions.

Tiğ oyasi refers to oyas made with the crochet hook. Because the double crochet stitch resembles the 'buttonhole' stitch of the *iğne oyasi*, it is easy to copy the needlemade technique using a very fine crochet hook and equally fine thread. Using the crochet techniques an oya can be made with a continuous thread much more quickly than using a needle and separate lengths of yarn – a similar process to the Venetian needlemade laces and Irish crochet laces in the last chapter. Oyas made with a crochet hook using beads with the thread are known as *boncuk oyasi*. Some are very beautiful, for example the *karabuk oyasi*. Oyas are also made by the tatting technique – these are known as *mekek oyasi*. Both crochet and tatted oyasi are either made separately or applied directly onto the fabric square – a crochet foundation would be required on the fabric for a tatted oyasi.

Oyas are also made with a hairpin, some using beads and some with sequins. The hairpin is used with a small crochet hook using the basic hairpin crochet techniques as explained in Chapter 14. The beads or sequins are threaded onto the yarn prior to starting

the oya. An oya made with the hairpin is usually made in two stages, firstly the making of the hairpin strip, then a line of chain stitches to make a firm and straight sewing on edge.

Oyas made separately would be worked in a sufficiently long length to surround a head square and sometimes you find a square with several centimetres without lace – the length of oya being too short. If the oya is to be worked directly onto the fabric, for example for the *tiğ oyasi*, a row of double crochet stitches with several chain stitches worked between the double crochet is made by inserting the fine crochet hook through the material. The edge of the fabric is previously hemmed, and the crochet makes a foundation for working either a *tiğ oyasi* or an *iğne oyasi*. Many oyas are starched when finished. This enables the petals of the flowers and leaves to be moulded in the hand as they dry.

Women from all backgrounds worked on the making of oyas using the various techniques mentioned. The women living on the farms in the countryside would work on their lace during the winter when they could not work outside, and the laces would be sold at the local market held either weekly or monthly. The extra money earned would supplement their income, and their work could be called a 'cottage industry'. The women of quality also made laces for pleasure and these pieces would not be sold; many would be given as presents. Oyas are still made today using the various techniques, and women can be seen working with their hooks in both the towns and the countryside.

The fabric used for the head squares is known as *tulbent* which is a material very suited to its use, that is, the square will lie perfectly on the head and never slip. The fibre is usually cotton; it is plain or patterned using the block printing technique and vegetable dyes. The finest old yemeni were silk, the colours plain black, a lovely bright green, yellow, pink or pale blue being popular. Today the fabric is thicker and slightly coarser, mostly cotton and often plain white. Some are still block printed. Often the oya is made from man-made yarn such as nylon. The women have great difficulty in buying the tiny beads and fine yarns which they like best, and this leads to thicker yarns made of nylon being used with the motifs further apart and fewer beads. Sometimes small pieces of fabric are used to take the place of the beaded motif.

Scarves form an important part of the female dress – they are worn to keep the hair clean while working in the house and while bathing, but perhaps of most importance as a protection from the sun. This is especially so if the hair is henna dyed. The scarves are sold in the markets and women are still seen wearing them today.

Sometimes oyas are used as a form of jewellery, and indeed, some of those illustrated would be very suitable for necklaces, bracelets and waist trimmings. Some needlemade and crochet techniques can be combined to make a flower brooch. The flower is made with a needle, and the leaves use a crochet hook and double crochet stitch.

428   A brooch using needlemade flowers and crochet
leaves. *Gift to author*

This chapter includes some suggested techniques for
making *tiğ oyasi* and *boncuk oyasi*, some using just the
crochet hook and some using the hairpin. See also
Chapter 14 on hairpin crochet. The choice of the hook
size, thickness of yarn and size of beads is of the
utmost importance. If you are learning how to work
the oyas for the first time, try the techniques using the
materials suggested. If you are using beads, it is
obvious that the size of hole in the bead will govern
the thickness of the yarn. For all examples using beads
as part of the oya, the beads are placed onto the yarn
prior to starting the oya. See figures 245, 246 in Chapter
9 for the method of transferring the beads onto the
working yarn.

Also illustrated are some ideas for dress decoration,
and decoration suitable for accessories using *tiğ oyasi*
and *boncuk oyasi*. In their own ethnic surroundings,
made in the traditional manner, oyas are exceedingly
beautiful and meaningful, expressing many thoughts.
They should be used with much thought, care and
appreciation.

Crochet was also used extensively in the making of
personal bags and purses. The examples seen varied
from about 150 years old to the present day. The very
finest examples were needlemade – using the same
technique as for the needlemade oya, and these bags
are very old. Purses used for money are known as *kese*
and many examples of these purses can be seen today
in personal collections. Money purses were made and
given as presents for special occasions, for example for
marriages. Purses were also given for good luck, and
some would contain sayings, such as *Masallah* –
meaning 'God willing'. This is rather a difficult word
to give a true translation of but that given is perhaps
the most appropriate. Many designs incorporated in
the work are symbolic or depict articles from the
surroundings. The designs being worked in different
colours.

429   A modern crochet bag using a man-made yarn in
red and gold trimmings – mostly chain stitches have
been used for this bag

Other designs on the kese incorporate such motifs as
the water jug (some say it is a dancing girl – the shape
being similar!), the cone form (*sanobesh*), flowers,
birds and cockerels. The crochet stitch used is the
double crochet, often working each stitch into the
single back loop for each double crochet stitch. The
crochet is worked in continuous circles, starting at the

tip, and increasing towards the opening. Some are
rectangular with straight sides, therefore no increasing would be required. The double crochet is very
closely worked, using fine threads and a small crochet
hook. All threads not being used when working a
pattern are worked over by the stitch in the yarn
being used, so no loops are left hanging on the wrong
side. Often oyas are seen decorating the edges of kese,
and decorative motifs and fringing can be seen on the
draw strings which close the purse.

430   Kese – worn on the belt. Several colours are used
for this tulip design. The tulip is a design for good
luck. The kese measures 14 cm long, 10 cm wide, the
tassel is 3 cm long, and there are two draw string cords
to close the kese. The kese is made in double crochet

throughout, the hook is placed into the back single loop, and worked in continuous circles. The crochet starts at the tip and is worked upwards. Tassels complete the kese.

431 The inside of the kese – the work is almost reversible. *Property of Mügül Andrews*

The other shapes of money purses are similar to the reticules used in England during the middle of the last century. The crochet reticule type seen in Turkey did not have metal rings, but contained a slit in the middle. The length varied from 35 to 45 cm depending on the length of the finishing tassels.

Most crochet bags use cotton or silk threads but some purses were made from fabric using pieces left over after making a dress. The construction of these bags is very inventive, imaginative and attractive.

Other crochet bags include the little containers made for men to carry their watch, seal and tobacco. Sometimes holders for letters and cigarette holders can be seen. A set of three such containers is a very collectable find.

Knitted socks formed an important part of the female costume in Turkey. These socks are hand knitted using very brightly coloured yarns, featuring geometric and floral designs. These socks are still made today and can be seen in the local shops and markets. Some of the old examples date back approximately 150 years.

The tops of the knitted socks feature a decorative edging which is very similar to the Bosnian braid illustrated in Chapter 5. Not all socks are finished with this type of crochet. The slip stitch is worked in continuous spirals, simply working round and round the top circumference of the sock. These examples are thought to come from Rumelli – the European part of the Ottoman Empire such as Bulgaria, Yugoslavia, Hungary and Albania. Gold threads with red, green and purple were popular colours for these edgings.

I have also seen crochet used for cushion covers. The crochet took the form of raised and stuffed motifs representing bunches of grapes with vine leaves and tendrils coiling around. The whole effect was similar to some Irish crochet work. The cover had not been made recently.

Some of the caps worn by the men while praying are made with the crochet hook using white cotton thread, and are very similar to those illustrated in Chapter 13.

Beaded oya of red berries (432 a and b) – Karabuk (Blackberry motif)

432 (a) Karabuk Oyasi using small red beads.

(a)

(b)

(c)

(b) Karabuk Oyasi using larger beads with a small 3 bead motif between the berries.
(c) Variation on (a) and (b) forming a grape like motif. Made by the author.

Select appropriate yarn, beads and hook size, eg Coats No. 40 mercer crochet yarn, ISR crochet hook – size 1.25; Beads 4 mm diameter.

Place beads on yarn first – 18 beads are required for each berry.

Work 10 chain for foundation.

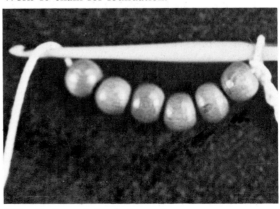

433 Push up 6 beads Loop A.

434   One chain

438   Place hook under yarn between 3rd & 4th bead of loop C.

435   Push up 6 beads, 1 chain Loop B.

439   Yarn over hook and draw through both loops

436   Push up 6 beads, 1 chain Loop C.
There are now 3 loops of 6 beads.

440   Insert hook into 4th chain from base of loop A.
441   Insert hook between 3rd & 4th bead of loop B.

437   3 chain.

442   Yarn over hook and draw through both loops on hook.

443   Insert hook between 3rd & 4th bead of loop A.

444 and 445   Yarn over hook and draw yarn up.

446   Yarn over hook and draw through both loops on hook.

One berry is complete.

3 double crochet stitches may be worked over the foundation chain at base of berry before working further foundation chain stitches prior to next berry.

Red-beaded oya – multiple loops (432c)

Suggested yarn: Coats No. 50. ISR crochet hook No. 1.50; Beads 2–3 mm diameter.

Place beads on yarn allowing 45 beads for each motif and 3 beads to be placed between motif.

Work 20 chain for foundation length.

*Push up 3 beads. 8 chain.

Yarn over hook 8 times. Push up 5 beads. Yarn over hook and draw through one loop. 1 chain.

(Push up 5 beads, yarn over hook and draw through two loops) 8 times.

8 chain*

* to * forms the repeat for this oya.

Cream and gold oya (447 and 448)

447   Oya using cream thread and small gold wooden beads.

Made by the author.

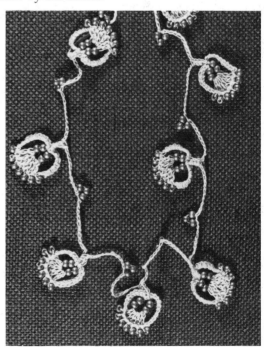

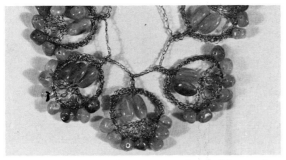

448   Same as 447 using copper wire and large glass beads.
Made by the author.
No. 1.75 ISR crochet hook; Coats No. 15 or 20; Beads 5 mm diameter.
*10 chain for base foundation. Push up 3 beads.
14 chain for base foundation. Push up 4 beads.
The motif:
Round 1   8 chain. 6 trebles between 2nd and 3rd bead of 4 bead group. 8 chain. Slip stitch to chain at base of 4 bead group. Circle shape now complete.
Round 2   10 double crochet over the 8 chain length. (Push up 1 bead, 1 double crochet in next treble) 7 times. 9 double crochet over 8 chain length. Slip stitch to first double crochet at start of the round. 4 double crochet over the base chain foundation to form a 'stem' to the motif.*
* to * forms the repeat for this edging.

Cream oya without beads (449 a)

449   (a) and (b)   Cream thread oyas with no beads. Two types of picots are shown: (a)   a loose treble; (b)   a pulled loop in double crochet. Made by the author.

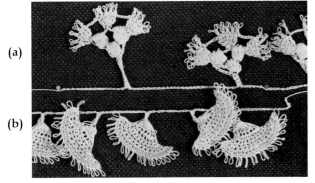

(a)

(b)

(a)   No. 1.75 ISR crochet hook; No. 20 Coats mercer crochet thread; A gauge for making loops (picots) such as a piece of piping cord, No. 1.00 10 cm long.
Work 30 chain.
The motif:
Start the fluted edge first:
Row 1   * ((Yarn over hook, place hook in front of gauge and take up yarn – 3 loops on hook – yarn over hook and draw through one loop, (yarn over hook and draw through 2 loops) twice)). Repeat from ((to)) 5 times. 5 chain.* Repeat from * to * 2 more times omitting 5 chain in last repeat. Turn work.

Row 2   3 chain to count as 1 treble. Yarn over hook, insert hook into 5th stitch from hook, yarn over hook and draw through yarn, yarn over hook and draw through one loop, yarn over hook and draw through 2 loops, (yarn over hook, insert hook into next stitch, yarn over hook and draw through yarn, yarn over hook and draw through 1 loop, yarn over hook and draw through 2 loops) 3 times. 5 loops on hook, yarn over hook and draw through all loops on hook. *4 chain. Miss 5 chain. Repeat from (to) 5 times. Yarn over hook and draw through all loops on hook*. Repeat from * to * once more. Miss 4 chain of original chain. 1 slip stitch over next chain. Turn work.
Row 3   1 slip stitch over next 3 chain. (*Yarn over hook, place hook in front of next 4 chain space, yarn over hook and extend loop to meet the stitch on hook,* repeat from * to * 10 times. Yarn over hook and draw through all loops on hook. 3 chain). Repeat from (to) once more, omitting 3 chain at end of repeat. 1 chain. Turn work.
Row 4   3 chain. Into the 3 chain space repeat * to * of Row 3 10 times, yarn over hook and draw through all loops on hook. 1 chain. Miss 4 chain of original chain. 1 double crochet into next 4 chain stitches.
This completes the motif.
Remove the piping cord gauge to form picots.
Work 30 chain stitches approximately between each motif.

Cream oya without beads (449 b)

No. 1.75 ISR crochet hook; No. 20 Coats mercer crochet thread; A gauge for making loops (picots) such as a piece of piping cord, No. 1.00 10 cm long.
** 14 chain.
Row 1   Extend stitch on hook to 1 cm. Make 1 chain. Make 5 half treble inserting the hook into second chain from hook, and extending the stitch on the hook to 1 cm. Turn work.
Row 2   1 chain, 1 double crochet into the second stitch from hook. 1 double crochet into next 3 stitches. 2 double crochet into next stitch. 1 double crochet into last stitch. Turn work.
Row 3   Repeat Row 2 working 1 double crochet into next 5 stitches (in place of 3 stitches). Turn work.
Row 4   Repeat Row 2 working 1 double crochet into next 7 stitches (in place of 3 stitches). Turn work.
Row 5   Repeat Row 2 working 1 double crochet into next 9 stitches (in place of 3 stitches). Turn work.
Row 6   1 chain. 1 double crochet into second stitch from hook. 1 double crochet into next stitch. (2 double crochet in next stitch, 1 double crochet in next stitch) 6 times. Turn work.
Row 7   Picot Row. 1 chain. Insert hook into second stitch from hook, yarn over hook and draw through yarn, yarn over hook and draw yarn through both loops on hook. Transfer stitch onto gauge. Remove hook. *Insert hook into single horizontal loop of stitch just made, yarn over hook and draw through yarn. Insert hook into next stitch of previous row, yarn over hook and draw through yarn. Yarn over hook and draw through both loops on hook. Transfer stitch onto gauge, remove hook*. Repeat from * to * to end of row.

Work 5 slip stitches down the side of the shape. Extend stitch to base of fan shape and work 1 slip stitch into the chain stitch at base. 1 chain. Work 4 double crochet over the chain foundation.**

Work approximately 20 chain stitches between motifs. Remove piping cord gauge.

** to ** completes the motif.

Flower oya (450)

450 Flower oya. A thicker yarn is used for the oya shown in 451 (c). Made by the author.

Suggested yarn: Coats No. 50 mercer crochet yarn. ISR crochet hook No. 1.50; Gauge – a piece of stiff card equal in width to 4 chain stitches.

Work 20 chain for foundation length between flowers.

The flower (using another yarn colour):

Round 1 Begin the centre of the flower as shown in figure 261, page 75. Work 5 chain to count as 1 long treble. Work 39 long trebles inserting the hook into centre of circle. Slip stitch to 5th chain at start of round. Close centre by pulling the cut end of yarn.

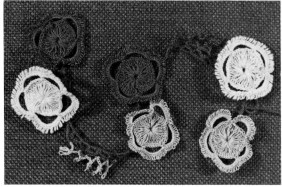

Round 2 (10 chain. Miss 7 stitches, 1 double crochet into next stitch) 4 times. 10 chain. Miss 7 stitches. Slip stitch into next double crochet.

Round 3 Into each 10 chain loop work 20 double crochet with looped picots as explained in example 449 (b). Join flowers to chain foundation as completed.

Note The long treble. Place gauge in front of chains against circle of yarn, yarn over hook and insert hook in front of gauge into centre of circle. Yarn over hook and draw up yarn. Yarn over hook and draw through one loop. (Yarn over hook and draw through 2 loops) twice. One long treble stitch completed. For working treble stitch over a gauge see figure 131, page 37.

Daisy flower oya using two colours in beads (451 a)

451 (a) Daisy oya using orange and white beads
(b) Fine oya using green beads with orange berry motifs
(c) Single flower shape – alternative variation using a bead in place of the looped picots as shown in 450. Made by the author

(a) Suggested yarn: Coats mercer crochet yarn No. 80 ISR crochet hook 0.75; White beads and orange beads 1 to 2 mm diameter.

Place beads on your thread in the following order: 5 orange beads for the centre, 18 white beads for petals and 3 bead loop between flowers, ending with 5 orange beads, 3 white beads.

Work *8 chain. Push up 3 white beads. 8 chain. Push up 5 beads in orange for centre. One chain.

Push up 3 white beads. 1 chain. 1 double crochet between 1st and 2nd bead of flower centre.

Push up 3 white beads. 1 chain. 1 double crochet between 2nd and 3rd bead of flower centre.

Repeat until 5 petals are complete.

Work 5 double crochet stitches on foundation chain below flower.*

* to * forms the repeat for this oya.

451

(a)

(b)

(c)

Beaded oya using green beads with orange berry motif (451 b)

Suggested yarn: Coats mercer crochet yarn No. 60–80. ISR crochet hook 1.00; orange beads and green beads 1–2 mm in diameter.

Place beads on yarn. Green beads on one spool. Orange beads on second spool.

Row 1 Using yarn with green beads. 10 chain for foundation length. *Push up 4 green beads. 7 chain.* Repeat * to * for required oya length.

Row 2 Using yarn with orange beads. 10 chain. 1 double crochet into 4th chain before first group of green beads. *4 chain. 1 slip stitch between 2nd and 3rd bead of 4 green bead group. Work 1 berry as shown in figure 432 (a). 4 chain. I double crochet into 4th chain from last group of green beads.* Repeat from * to * to complete Row 1.

451 (c) is worked in the same way as 450, placing one bead in place of the picots.

Oya with white thread and small orange beads (452)

452 An unusual oya using tiny orange beads and a fine white thread. Made by the author

Coats No. 80 mercer crochet yarn, No. 1.00 ISR crochet hook; beads 1–2 mm in diameter. Place beads on yarn.

*8 chain, push up 3 beads for small motif. 8 chain.
The large motif:
12 chain. (Push up 5 beads, 1 chain. Push up 1 bead, 1
chain) 4 times. Join with a slip stitch to the first loop
made. Work in continuous spirals round the chain
length in double crochet, inserting the hook into the
stitches forming the circle of beads. There should be 8
stitches to each round. Continue working round the
chain length until 8 rows are complete with 64 beads
in total.
Work 3 double crochet over the chain length at base of
barrel shape, working the third double crochet into
the 9th chain from last group of 3 beads forming the
small motif.* Repeat from * to * for required length of
oya.
Working note:
1   Wrap the yarn round the little finger several times
to keep the tension very tight and control the beads.
2   Make sure that the group of 4 loops with the 5
beads in each loop, is placed away from you as you
work, and the chain length is placed towards you.
Insert the hook into the next stitch – the back single
loop – yarn over hook and draw through yarn. Place 1
bead against the hook, yarn over hook and draw
through both loops on hook, thus placing the beads
around the chain length.

Oya using two yarns and beads (453)

453   Oya worked over a base foundation cord with
beads. Made by the author
Yarn A. No. 2 piping cord or string of similar
thickness.
Yarn B. Twilley's *Twenty*, or Coats No. 5 mercer
crochet thread.
Crochet hook No. 2.50 ISR. Wooden beads 6 mm in
diameter.
Place the beads onto yarn B.
Work over yarn A for every double crochet (see figure
230, page 64).
4 double crochet. Place 2 beads against yarn A, 1
chain.

*5 double crochet. (Push up 1 bead, 1 chain. 1 double
crochet) 3 times.
2 double crochet. Push up 2 beads, 1 chain. 1 double
crochet. Turn work.
1 double crochet between the 2 beads forming the
centre row.
7 double crochet. Push up 2 beads, 1 chain. 6 double
crochet. Push up 2 beads, 1 chain. 1 double crochet.
Turn work. 1 double crochet between the two beads
forming the centre row.*
Repeat from * to * for the required length.
To secure loops work a length of chain stitches
between each pair of beads, working 1 double crochet
between the two beads on edge of loop with 6 chain
stitches between each double crochet.

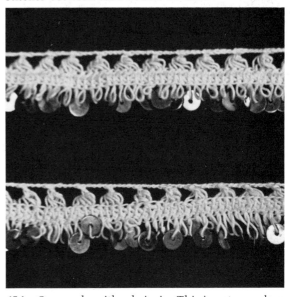

454   Oya made with a hairpin. This is not a modern
piece. This is known as a *pul oyasi* because of the
sequins – *pul* refers to the disc or sequin shape. The
braid is 1.5 cm deep. The sequins are placed on the
thread prior to starting the oya. One sequin is placed
on alternate loops on one side of the braid only. On the
side without the sequins 4 loops are joined together by
chain stitches to form a firm and straight sewing on
edge. *Property of Mügül Andrews*

Cream oya with wooden beads (455 and 456)

455 Beaded oya worked with larger beads using the hairpin technique

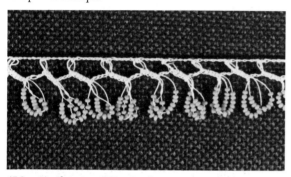

456 Similar to 455. Explanatory notes given in Chapter 14 on hairpin work.

Size 20 mm hairpin prong. Coates No. 50 mercer crochet thread.

Wooden beads 6 mm in diameter. No. 1.00 ISR crochet hook.

Place beads on yarn.

Make 10 chain to start foundation.

Hold the hook with the loop of the last chain on the hook, in centre of prong. Wind the yarn round the right hand prong front to back, and work 1 chain. (Push up 7 beads against hook, turn prong clockwise, 1 chain. Turn prong clockwise placing yarn round left prong, 1 double crochet under the back single loop of yarn on left prong, ie the loop with the beads) twice. Push up 7 beads, turn prong, 1 chain. 3 double crochet over *all* loops on left hand prong, 1 double crochet *through* all three loops on left hand prong. Turn prong clockwise. 4 chain.

*(push up 7 beads, turn prong clockwise, 1 chain. Turn prong clockwise, 1 double crochet under left prong) twice. Push up 7 beads, turn prong clockwise, 1 chain. 3 double crochet under *all* loops of left hand prong, 1 double crochet *through* 2 loops of left hand prong. Turn prong clockwise. 4 chain.*

Repeat from * to * for length required.

To secure loops without beads, work a length of chain stitches between each group of 3 loops, working 1 double crochet into the loops and 4–5 chain between each double crochet.

457 A scarf illustrating the beaded oyas. *Property of Mügül Andrews*

458 Patchwork leather jerkin trimmed with a modified beaded oya

459   The oya combined with tucks and lace to give a
rich textured surface

460   Individual crochet motifs and frills

461   Garment ideas combining strips of different
crochet patterns and fastenings

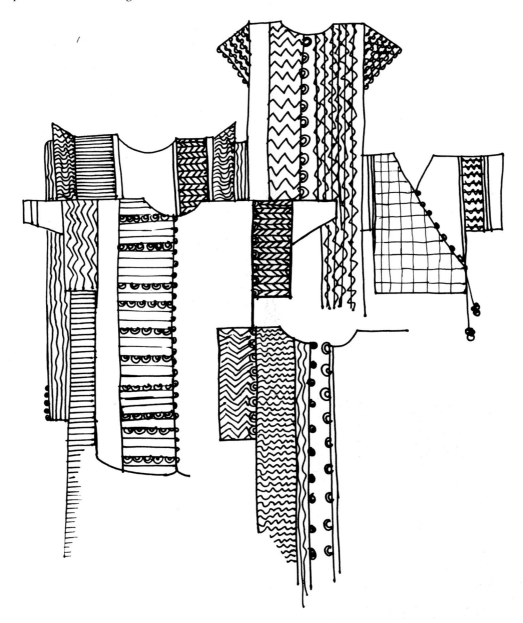

Further reading
Books referring to Turkish crochet include:
Celal Esad Arseven, *Les Arts Decoratifs Turcs*,
Istanbul.
S F A Caulfeild, *Encyclopedia of Victorian Need-
lework*, first published by A W Cowan in 1882 under
the title *The Dictionary of Needlework: An Encyclopedia
of Artistic, Plain and Fancy Needlework*.
Mrs Palliser, *A History of Lace*, first published 1902.
   Some examples can be seen in the private collec-
tions of the Yapi ve Kredi Bank in Istanbul.

References

1   The *Ashley Book of Knots* refers to the chain sinnet (ie the chain foundation) as: monkey chain, monkey braid, single trumpet cord, single bugle cord, chain stitch, crochet stitch, chain braid.

2   The gauge can be a large hairpin prong used in hairpin crochet. Otherwise two knitting needles placed into two pieces of wood, with holes the same size as the needles, make a very workable gauge. The spaces between the knitting needles is 6.5 cm in this sample.

3   Barbara Snook, *Embroidery Stitches*, page 57.

4   See S F A Caulfeild, *Encyclopedia of Victorian Needlework*.

5   Sizes of the various hairpin prongs available: 10 mm 15 mm 20 mm 25 mm 30 mm 40 mm 50 mm 60 mm 80 mm 100 mm ($\frac{1}{2}$in.–4in.) approximately.

Old types of prongs with more than one prong can sometimes be found in antique shops. These prongs produce multiple loops and varying lengths of fringing.

6   Paper patterns made by following the directions in Winifred Aldrich, *Metric Pattern Cutting*.

7   Elizabeth Boyle, *The Irish Flowerers*, page 50.

8   S F A Caulfeild, *Encyclopedia of Victorian Needlework*, page 102.

9   Pat Earnshaw, *The Identification of Lace*, page 22.

10   Annette Feldman, *Handmade Lace and Patterns*, page 11.

11   Sylvia Groves, *The History of Needlework Tools and Accessories*, page 100.

12   Mrs Palliser, *A History of Lace*, and Pat Earnshaw, *The Identification of Lace*.

13   Mrs Palliser, *A History of Lace*, page 445.

Suppliers

All yarns are available at good department stores and wool shops throughout the country.

Fred Aldous Ltd
P O Box 135
37 Lever Street
Manchester M60 1UX
Many craft materials

Creative Beadcraft Ltd
Denmark Works
Sheep Cote
Dell Road
Beamont End
Nr Amersham
Buckinghamshire HP7 0RX
Beads by mail order

Ells and Farrier Ltd
5 Princes Street
London W1
*Beads and fancy yarns, tambour
hooks and holders –
personal shoppers only*

**The Handweavers' Studio
and Gallery Ltd**
29 Haroldstone Road
London W17 7AN

John Lewis Partnership Ltd
Oxford Street
London W1
Folkwear Ethnic Patterns

Harrods Ltd
Knightsbridge
London SW1

MacCulloch and Wallis Ltd
25–26 Dering Street
London W1R 0BH

Mace and Nairn
89 Crane Street
Salisbury
Wiltshire SP1 2PY
Yarns and fine lace threads

Silken Strands
33 Linksway
Gatley
Cheadle
Cheshire SK8 4LA
A selection of unusual yarns

Elizabeth Tracy
45 High Street
Haslemere
Surrey

Bibliography

Aldrich, Winifred, *Metric Pattern Cutting*, Mills
    and Boon 1976
Anderson, Rosemarie, *Crochet for the Connoisseur*,
    Batsford 1979
Caulfeild, S F A and Saward, Blanche A,
    Encyclopedia of Victorian Needlework, first
    published 1882, facsimile reprint Hamlyn, 1972
Crafts magazine, the Crafts Council
Davenport, Elsie G, *Your Handspinning*, Select
    Books, California, 1955
de Dillmont, Therese, *Encyclopedia of Needlework*,
    DMC, 1897
Fashion and Craft magazine, Forbes Publications
Green, David, and Ashburner, Jenni, *Dyes from the
    Kitchen*, Batsford 1979

Groves, Sylvia, *The History of Needlework Tools and
    Accessories*, first published Hamlyn 1966,
    reprinted David and Charles 1973
Hitz Edson, Nicki, and Stimmel, Arlene, *Creative
    Crochet*, Nelson 1975
Leadbeater, E. *Handspinning*, Studio Vista 1976
Nordford, Jill, *Needle Lace and Needleweaving*,
    Studio Vista 1974
Norton, Maggi Jo, *Crochet Designs from Simple
    Motifs*, Batsford 1978
Pitt Feldman, Del, *The Crocheter's Art*,
    Nelson, 1975
Snook, Barbara, *Embroidery Stitches*, Batsford 1963
Walters, James, *Crochet Workshop*, Sidgwick and
    Jackson 1979

Index

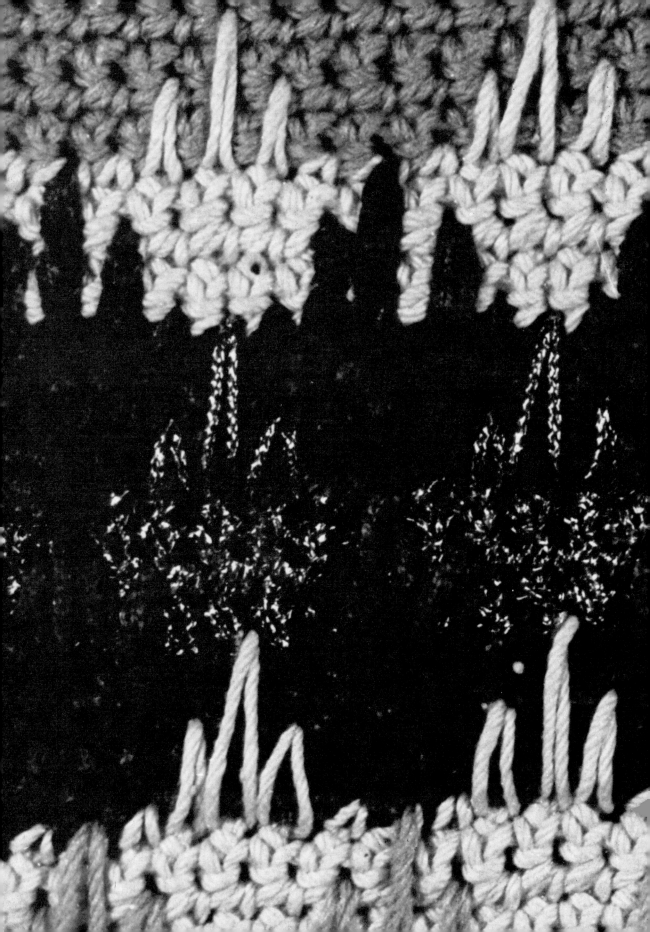

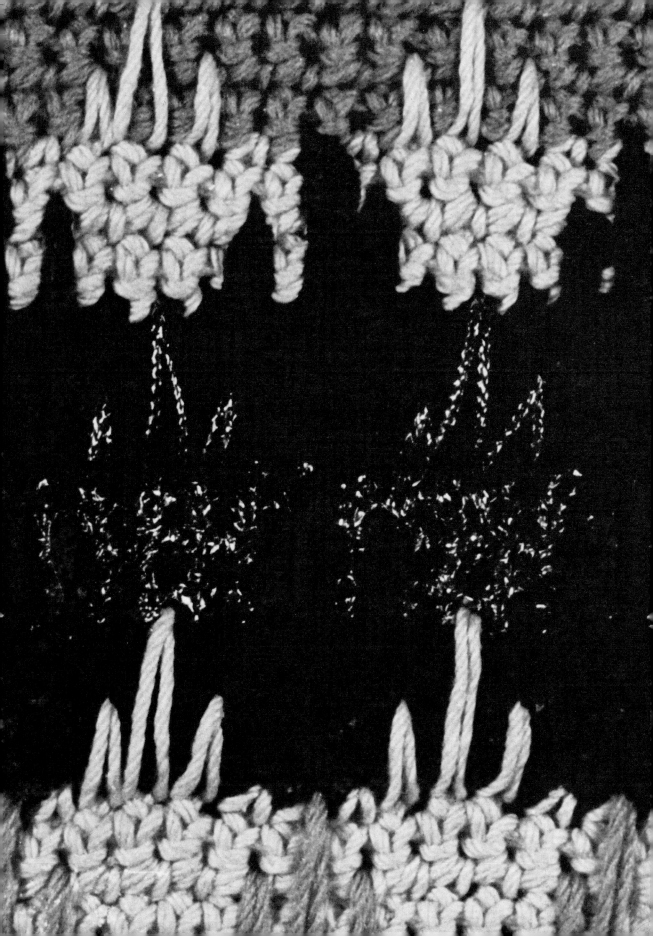